M000119703

Nils Christie

Beyond Loneliness
and Institutions

Nils Christie

Beyond Loneliness and Institutions
Communes for Extraordinary People

Wipf & Stock
PUBLISHERS
Eugene, Oregon

Wipf and Stock Publishers
199 W 8th Ave, Suite 3
Eugene, OR 97401

Beyond Loneliness and Institutions
Communes for Extraordinary People
By Christie, Nils
Copyright©1989 Universitetsforlaget
ISBN 13: 978-1-55635-596-7
ISBN 10: 1-55635-596-3
Publication date 8/30/2007
Previously published by Universitetsforlaget, 1989

Preface to the 2001 Edition

What this book is about?

It is about a social system where they decided to disregard money as an incentive for work and as indicator of a person's prestige and worth. They put all money in one hat, and use it according to need.

It is about a social system where they decided that some tools were dangerous for social life and therefore banned from use within the system.

It is about a social system where they decided that some classificatory categories—e.g., insanity and retardation—were disruptive for social life and therefore to be avoided. Other dangerous categories, and therefore also banned, are such as director or boss. Instead all living there are villagers or co-workers. This does not mean they are all equal in daily life. Some have more power. But that power is to a greater extent related to who they are—and how they behave—as persons, not to their formal status in the system.

These villagers all live together in the same houses, they go to work in the village and share cultural activities inside the village.

These are systems that might have been called "total institutions," a label describing a phenomenon much despised in the literature on such matters. But I want to go even one step further in what is usually seen as negative characterisation; I am willing to call these social systems "ghettos." And I say so with honorary intentions.

Ghettos proved fatal in nazi- and fascist-times. But that must not lead us to forget the values in some types of ghetto-life—a gathering of people supposed to be similar due to race, or actually being similar by history or joint culture. They may be forced into extraordinary co-operation by external threats or by someone's extraordinary burning ideas or revelations. It might be a terrible place to live, if you break some of the basic rules for life. But it is also and at the same time a place of life with an amount of experienced security and vibrant intensity in interaction deeply missed in daily life for most of us. Those ever touched by life in a good ghetto will never, ever, adapt fully to non-ghetto life.

*   *   *

The book was first published in 1989. What has happened later? Elèuthera[1] asked me to write a preface and tell. I resisted, but they insisted. And they were right. But it is a difficult task, if done seriously. It is a difficult task, because the main feature of what has happened since I wrote the book is that nothing principally new has happened. It has been a period of stability, not of change.

Why is a non-change more difficult to describe than change? Because it is against the spirit of the time and therefore so easily will be interpreted as a defect.

*   *   *

A domineering idea in our culture is to go out and shape all societies into our picture. So also with modernity.

It was in 1949 that Harry Truman launched the campaign for fighting underdevelopment, changing the globe into one for a family of highly industrialised nations. The poor of the third world were to be rescued from their underdevelopment and poverty. It was a forceful ideology, presuming that the good life was the one lived according to the standards dominated by economic rationality.

But it was at the same time an ideal, which meant that all nations ought to develop into our model, with our simplified goal-structure. The concept *underdevelopment* has been dropped. Today the correct designation is *countries of the third world*, but the realities are the same. Countries of the third world are to be helped up to our level; their third-class wagons are to be rebuilt, to be like ours at first class. To get this done, these countries have to change one essential feature; from being multi-institutional, they have to become mono-institutional. They will then, *as nations*, be able to work themselves out of their situation of international dependency. But at the same

---

1. Elèuthera is the publishing company that released the Italian version of this book, *Oltre la solitudine e le istituzioni. Comunità per gente fuori norma* (2001), in which this preface originally appeared.

time—and this is not commented on in the recipe for social transformation—they will move into a situation where a considerable number of citizens are brought into a situation of *individual* dependency. Or, in another picture, underdeveloped countries are dependent on the highly developed countries to obtain an increase in the national product, but at the same time they are in all their underdevelopment very often organised in ways where there is a place for all people, where there is a need for all hands. Helped out of underdevelopment, this is all turned upside down. The *national* dependency on other states is exchanged for the *individual* dependency on one's own. These societies move into the category of nations of producers and consumers, but then, according to the logic in the age of automatisation and rationalisation, a great number of their inhabitants will soon come in the situation where they lose full participation in the activities seen as the only important ones—the activities of production and consumption.

Ivan Illich[2] says:

> Well into the industrial age, for most people living in subsistence cultures, life was still predicated on the recognition of limits that just could not be transgressed. Life was bounded within the realm of immutable necessities. The soil yielded only known crops; the trip to the market took three days; the son could infer from the father what his future would be. . . . [N]eeds, meaning necessities, had to be endured . . . . In a moral economy of subsistence, the existence of desires is taken as much for granted as the certainty that they could not be stilled. (90)

One lived the life that was. One had wishes, but then in the form of hope, not as need based on rights. The human being is, in the perspective of Illich, transformed from *homo sapiens* (the wise or tasteful human) into *homo miserabilis*.

Seen like this, the idea of development is an imperialistic idea, imperialistic in the arrogance of the highly developed nations—we are helping you to be as we are. And imperialistic in the fact that the help consists of encouragement and/or coercion to force these nations from a multi-institutional organisation into a mono-institu-

---

2. Ivan Illich, "Needs," in *The Development Dictionary: A Guide to Knowledge as Power*, edited by Wolfgang Sachs, 88–101, London: St. Martin's, 1992.

tional one by letting ideas and values from one institution colonise the others.

*   *   *

Vidaråsen and the other villages represent a type of life where they have not succumbed to the pressure of development. They have refused to modernise. They have analysed the values of the old societies, made themselves aware of them, and reorganised life in accordance to these values.

So, this is the problem when describing later developments.

Nothing much has happened since the first edition. And why should it? Village life is a slow rhythm: birth, ageing, death, and the arrival of some newcomers for a year or for life. Some new buildings, some restoration of old ones, but mostly life has continued, life as usual. It has continued as village life in the old form.

But then comes the next and challenging question: How is this possible? How to explain non-development in a globe filled with belief in progress?

I have no certain answers, but some suggestions. First comes the emphasis on the villagers as the reference point for all major activities in the villages. Several of those living there have troubles in walking; that puts limits to the size of the area covered by the villages. The same effect has the unwillingness to accept bureaucratic hierarchies. Such forms are difficult to prevent if size is increased. The elimination of money as an incentive is also a factor. It is nothing to earn. Development might easily be seen as a threat against life qualities—more people to relate to, less time for close contacts.

But still, many of those living in the villages have grown up in "normal society." They have been socialised to the goal of progress; they have been trained to get a job, a family, advance socially as well as economically, maybe create a firm for themselves—all the usual signs of success. Why do they stay on? Why do they not change the villages into modern nursing homes of one sort or another?

I believe that the major reason is that the villages are filled with *alternative* challenges. If you live close to a human without an ordinary language, it is an enormous victory if you one day manage to understand the body language of that person and later continuously advance in that understanding. If a person who never walked alone between two houses one day performed such an act of heroism, it is an act that fills much of the day with joy. In addition come all the other social rewards connected with ghetto living. There are many stabilisers in village life.

But still, it might have gone wrong. The villages might have been destroyed by their economic situation. Not by lack of money, but because their surplus!

I have already mentioned their basic arrangement with all money in one hat, and I give the details in the general text. What I here in the preface need to mention, is that this principle gives the villages the possibility to become relatively affluent social systems. The villages receive less money from the Norwegian state than other systems with so many persons with extraordinary difficulties would have received. But people living here have no private economy. The village is their home. They do not have to buy houses, cars, insurance. Therefore much of the money remains in the hat. And from that hat it is used: for renovating houses, for new horses, for buying more land, for building a new hall for celebrating, for building new houses for new villagers. And here is the threat. The money might have been used to an over-expansion, to extra rewards to particularly deserving villagers—rewards which might have threatened the egalitarian standards inside the village, or to a general living standard so high above the usual for Norway that trouble might have followed. The very stability of the villages might be endangered, not by too little money, but by too much.

The problem has been solved by generosity. The most remarkable that has happened since I wrote my book, has been an enormous expansion of the village movement in Eastern Europe. Four new villages have been established: one in Russia, one in Estonia, one in Poland, and most recently one in Lithuania. All of them have received major assistance from the Norwegian villages in the form of money, buildings, equipment, and personnel. Observing this development, I was in the first years rather hesitant and feared that the Norwegian villages over-stretched themselves. Money and manpower was needed inside the Norwegian villages; it was dangerous to send it all to the East.

I was wrong. I should have remembered the institution of Potlatch. Or I should have remembered other cases described by social anthropologists, cases where surplus was destroyed, sent away, or redistributed so that the basic structure of the tribe or the community was not changed or destroyed. Helping to create villages in Eastern Europe has made villages in Norway able to preserve their identity. The entrepreneurial drive got a non-destructive outlet. The surplus has been used for good purposes. It has been development, but development meaning more villages, more examples of alternative ways of living. And this in nations where these alternatives are highly needed in competition with the ordinary Westernised ideas now penetrating the East with the message of the blessings of economic competition and development.

Nils Christie
Oslo, Norway
December 30, 2000

Contents

Preface

This is a book about some experimental villages for extraordinary people. Experimental in having a shared economy and communal living. Experimental in providing room for most sorts of people with a rich variety of eccentric behaviour. Experimental in reconstructing ancient social and cultural forms. Most sorts of people – many seen as "deficient" by the state classificatory system – here share all life conditions; house, meals, work, cultural life. No individual salary, no staff, no clients. The villages are not institutions, but they are not examples of ordinary life either.

I have had some sort of association with these villages for 20 years, and have moved back and forth between them and life in the ordinary society. Each move has been a cultural and emotional shock. Two types of life. Two types of reasons for life. Through their differences the two illuminate each other. This book is an attempt to describe what becomes visible – on both sides.

The task throughout the book will be threefold.

First, to describe the villages and try to understand what sort of rare species they represent. There are between 50 and 60 such villages in Europe today, and also some on other continents. It is of theoretical importance to know them more systematically. Industrialized societies, both in the East and the West, have in their efficiency also been efficient in extinguishing alternative social arrangements. The number of tribes shrink, variation diminishes. But in the middle of all this, new forms with new radical alternatives develop. New species appear. They offer new opportunities for the understanding of social life.

Secondly, experimental villages in the midst of our societies are to some extent nurtured by dissatisfaction with our major solutions. These exceptional social arrangements might thereby also prove exceptionally well suited to illuminating problematic aspects of modern industrialized societies.

Thirdly comes the question whether these villages might be of exemplary value, particularly if ideas from the villages might be of any help in the present crisis in social work. Institutions are torn down everywhere. The expressed goal is to get those who are different back to ordinary society. This raises the question of what sort of life extraordinary people will get in the ordinary society. Materially it will be an acceptable life, at least in states of welfare solidarity. But will it be good enough when evaluated according to criteria of richness in social participation and cultural life? And will it be a life in social forms where the extraordinary qualities of extraordinary people are enabled to influence the ordinary society, to make that society into a better society, also for ordinary people? These are the themes for the last part of the book.

I write in English, to me a foreign language. Words do not come fluently; they have to be carved out. It has its costs, rich material might be unduly condensed. But brevity also has advantages. So has also the extra effort needed. In the struggle to find the right formulations, words get a sort of physical quality. The struggle also helps to create distance from the phenomena described and, I hope, also honesty in the description. What can easily be disguised by the help of the mother-tongue, remains naked and vulnerable after the slow process of carving.

A final note on language: Mine is not "proper Oxford English". Most of us using English are not English. Why pretend to be, and adhere to sophisticated standards not ours, particularly since this often mystifies the content? The world-wide use of English is a result of a long historical development. I will act as if England has lost her property right to her language and use my share of the inheritance as I find suitable and in harmony with the pulse of my Norwegian.

The book is to a large extent the result of a joint effort. Most major points in the text have been described to and discussed with those living in the villages. Often they have brought me to a deeper understanding. On a few points some of them will disagree with my interpretations. The final responsibility is therefore mine. But often I am no more than their voice.

My gratitude also goes to friends and colleagues for constructive criticism of some of the major ideas, and of various drafts of the manuscript. Of great help have been Flemming Balvig, Vigdis Christie, Stan Cohen, Liv Finstad, Cecilie Høigård, Ivan Illich, Tom Lockney, Maeve McMahon, Annick Prieur, and Anne Sæterdal. Two persons have had a particular impact on the ideas in this book: Margit Engel, a major source for ideas and initiatives in village life, and Hedda Giertsen, who through practice and analysis has helped to clarify some major dimensions in social life.

Astri Horgen has provided exceptional help in getting the manuscript into shape, and has also kept my deviant language within certain borders. So has Ronald Walford in the last stage of the manuscript. But last as well as first: It is the extraordinary people in the villages who have been my main teachers.

Oslo, June 1989
Nils Christie

1

Five Arenas

Januz Korczak was a Polish Jew. He was a great story-teller for children, a medical doctor, and the director of a home for orphans in Warsaw. When the children were sent to an extermination camp, he was given the option to leave for another destination. His choice was to stay with the children. In *Vidaråsen* they gave his name to one of the houses, up on a small hill.

From the windows in this house one can see most of the village. The barn and the greenhouses are close to the centre of the village, with the workshops spread around. A bit more on the periphery we see houses for ordinary living, all built in wood, which is the usual building material in Norway.

There are five such villages in the country. *Vidaråsen* is the "mother village", twenty years old, situated in the southern part of the country, half an hour's drive from Tønsberg, a local town now, but a capital in Viking times. In Vidaråsen there live 150 people, 12 cows and calves, one horse, 30 hens, 20 sheep and an unknown number of cats. Elks are often visitors during winter-nights, as are also deer, hares and foxes. Vidaråsen has a bakery which produces for sale, a carpenter's shop, a pottery, one workshop for making dolls, earlier also one for making candles, a wood workshop, and a farm and two greenhouses run according to bio-dynamic principles. What all this means – and also what social consequences it brings – will be described when the time is ripe. The most impressive building in Vidaråsen is the "Hall", a huge building for all sorts of social occasions, lectures, plays, village meetings and concerts. Three hundred people can be seated in the Hall. Musicians like to play there, because of the quality of the acoustics and because of the quality of the listeners. The village also has a chapel and a combined cafeteria and shop.

The surroundings of Vidaråsen are in contrast to some stereotypes of how Norway ought to look: no spectacular views, only small hills, a brook, but no lakes. From this perspective it is a relief to come to the next village, two hours' drive northwards, a bit up the valley-side with an impressive view of small towns, forests, and then mountains far away to the west. Further up behind this village is a great forest. Here you can walk for days before you reach the next house. This is the home district of "trolls" and "hulders", – fantasy figures from times long past. Asbjørnsen and Moe – the Norwegian equivalents of the Grimm brothers – strolled these forests, listened to the locals and published what they found proper enough to appear in print. The name of this village is *Solborg/Alm*. Here live 50 people and the usual number of animals. Vegetables, and a metal-workshop, play a particularly important part in the production. The village has a weaving workshop and a joinery, and also runs a school and a kindergarten, both for ordinary children.

Hogganvik is situated on the west coast of Norway. The fiord is there, just where the garden ends. On sunny days it looks like an exaggerated tourist brochure. But most days are rainy. Humid air from England hits the hills just behind Hogganvik and falls as acid rain on the 45 people and the cows and calves which live there. Hogganvik was the biggest farm in the district. By now one house has been added, but not so many as they need. The west coast of Norway is the homeland of strong believers that their belief in God is the only possible form. The village variant is not easily accepted. This means trouble and concretely reduced opportunities for all sorts of expansions of the village.

This has not been the situation further north. *Jøssåsen* is situated close to the mountains – 300 metres above sea level, which is a lot when you come that far north. Fruits cannot grow there, and of vegetables only the roughest. Here 40 people live, farm the land, and work in shops. This village is warmly embraced by the local community. These are communities struggling against losing their population. The village meant new vitality for the district. Norway is also so formed that the level of spontaneity increases the further north one moves. It is a sort of opposite to Italy.

Vallersund is the last village in this family of five. Far out on a peninsula in the North Sea, an old harbour for the fishing boats from the time when they went north each winter to catch cod, or for the traditional and important trade with Russian boats. Fish from Norway, grain from Russia. The major building in the village is from somewhere in the 1700s; a small store is preserved from a bit later, so is also a special grain-bank – a reserve for black years without fish or years with war and blockade. But the village has added new houses. High above flies a windmill, the highest in Norway and with a capacity sufficient to sell surplus electricity to the municipal electricity company.

Today 30 people live in Vallersund. Workshops are less developed; building activities have up to now absorbed most energy. In addition to farming, fishing is a natural activity here. Oyster production has just started.

We shall soon get to know more about these villages. But let us first move closer to those living there.

2

Village People

2.1 Like most people

Meals are seldom occasions for food only. Meals are for social
life. Where several people live together, meals thus become important social arenas. News is distributed, emotions exposed, with
tender touches, angry words. Meals give opportunities. One of
them is to present oneself to others exactly as one hopes to be
seen.

The presentation of oneself is often intensified when there are
guests at the table. Guests arrive with blank minds. There the old-
timers at the table can present themselves as they most want to be
seen.

I had trouble with one of the persons in one of the houses in
one of the villages. His voice was loud and continuously in use.
He exerted a sort of monopoly of sound, competing voices had no
chance. And guests increased his output. Often they liked it, listened, nodded, encouraged him to continue. Not only story A and
B, but also C and D. The permanent members of the household
could have killed the guests for giving encouragement. Lots of
participants had potential contributions, maybe something new, at
a minimum their own need for self-presentation. And story A and
B and C and D were familiar to them down to their most minute
detail, because the stories were repeated in exactly the same way
each time. There were no more stories than these four, but they
lasted throughout the meal if the monopoly of sound-producing
was not brought to an end after story B or C.

When the meaning of these stories came to light, it became
easier to live with them. The producer was, and is, a stout, self-
confident looking man. His bodily posture is in itself a good intro-
duction – strong and industrious, a good worker, third generation
in the same craft, a pillar of village life, one to be trusted. And
this presentation through his body is completely correct. It is one

of the key persons in the village who narrates the stories from A to D.

But the teller has a problem. He cannot read. He cannot write. He cannot participate in any ordinary conversation. When he makes an attempt, it all ends in a mess. But he – and this is in contrast to most other people in the village – puts a great emphasis on *being like most people*. That is what his brother is. That is what his sister is, so much that she will not accept any visit from her brother in the village; she finds it embarrassing. The sound monopolist at the table knows it all, the general ideals, how he fails, how his sister looks at it. The good thing is to be normal.

Then come the guests. From A to D the story-teller presents himself as a man equal to all others. Seen in this light his stream of words is part of one large cover-up. Strange? Typical of handicapped people? Join me on a tour to Israel, and I will try to answer.

2.2 Vulnerability

The day was a hot one in Jerusalem. The air quivered around the University buildings up on the hill. I am late, I am to meet my friend up there, and have to catch a bus to be on time. Mount Scopus is the name of the University of Jerusalem, but how does that name look in Hebrew? I dared to ask an unknown lady, that was a victory, but defeat was soon to follow. I misunderstood her answer, heard her shout when the bus-doors shut behind me. Had to change to a new bus, sweating embarrassment; at last the University, but then the next ordeal; the long row of office doors. Again only signs in Hebrew. Perfect memory is needed where illiteracy reigns. Where is his office, was it not the fifth to the left, vis-à-vis the fire extinguisher? I am not sure, only that next to my friend is a man I do not want to meet that day. The Hebrew signs are large and beautiful. I have to act. Try door number five. Catastrophe – exactly the person I did not want to meet. Next door. New catastrophe. My friend has gone. Seek consolation in the cafeteria. As usual I don't understand the menu, ask for something unknown, pay with a large note to evade lots of sounds which probably mean I ought to pay more. An old trick among tourists and other handicapped persons. Shrewdness is needed when one is without words. But the cashier turns sour. Walk to town to evade once more having to ask for the right bus. Contemplate making a detour to the Wailing Wall, but this seems too far in the heat. Complain instead to empty air of being lost in a life where I cannot read, cannot write, cannot even talk to most of those around me. Back to my own door. Gesticulate with the carpenter in the backyard. An agreeable man, I think. Let myself in. Safe again. Get a glimpse of myself in the mirror. Good to see someone who knows me. Who knows I am quite ordinary.

2.3 To rest in oneself

Cover-operations absorb energy – always from the major actor, sometimes from the surroundings. Confident people are people who to a large extent appear as they are. Therefore, it was good to hear about a telephone conversation one day in the village. A youngster phoned the bus station from the village. He wanted to know about the bus departures. The answer became too complicated, and he exclaimed: "No, you must slow down. I am mentally retarded, you know."

Or Anna. We had a quarrel, and in the excitement it slipped out of me: "Are you quite dumb?" Anna shot back: "Yes, that is why I am here."

Or Helge. Most days he walks around in the village with a small briefcase. In this he has a note-pad, and on the pad he often writes. Page after page. On big occasions he nearly always gives a speech. His presentation is short, precise, warm, and often funny. It becomes a real celebration when Helge has spoken. Great ovations follow, applause given in gratitude and joy. The problem with his speeches is only that they are nearly completely without words. In direct conversation it is possible to recognize words, but the speeches on the big occasions are different. They have a beautiful rhythm. They are perfect in form, firm, but with melody, just as his written notes. The notes are also clear in form, but completely without letters and words. Helge's statements come from the heart, and enter hearts. The village likes to listen to him and understands important parts of his message. Helge's statements are high on content and low on words. So often in life it is the other way around.

2.4 There are two Leif's in the village

They live in the same house, in the same room. It might have been easier if they had also lived in the same body.

Leif One is a stout, self-determined do-it-at-once man. A do-gooder might have been the term if it had not been for the fact that so many of his acts turned out badly. He walks, talks and acts as one of those self determined businessmen that run the modern world. He talks continuously, is engaged in all sorts of problems in the village, asks for the floor during all village meetings, initiates reforms.

Leif Two is a soft-spoken, shy person. He rings the village-bell. You can rely on him. The bell sounds exactly when it is supposed to and as it is supposed to. It sounds good. If Leif is away, there is not the same musicality in the air of Vidaråsen. He works in and around the greenhouse. Quiet, not quick, but more than sufficient. He likes small talk, but does not ask for the floor in the village meetings.

Last night Leif One hit Leif Two with a bottle. He hit him in the face and fled the room. I entered seconds later, and found Leif Two stretched out on a couch. It looked bad, particularly to me since I had not recognized that his two eyes are always uncoordinated. He was up after a few minutes, receiving warm greetings from everybody.

The encounter took place in the cafeteria. Twice a week this is an arena for social life, but fights had to my knowledge never occurred. Acts of physical violence are rare in Vidaråsen, as in the country generally. When it happens, the shock is great. The villagers were upset. A man like Leif One could not remain in the village. At least he ought to be banned from the cafeteria, and be severely punished. Thor promised to carry out that necessary step next day. I intervened, suggesting that the perpetrator maybe had punished himself sufficiently through the same act. Thor agreed, but repeated his promise in another circle when we were all about to leave.

Why did it happen?

Maybe we shall one day receive a profound answer. But on the surface it is simple enough: The house-parents were away. Each time they leave, Leif One loses control. It is close to a natural law:

Cutting the electric wire to the house
Cutting the telephone line
Cutting the gas-pipe
and now the bottle attack

I met him early next morning. Thor, who last night swore he
would punish him, promised now in a whisper not to interfere.
Maybe he sensed he could not torture Leif more than Leif could
torture himself. Continuously Leif mumbled: "I should not have
done it, I should not . . ." I am afraid he did not even hear the
morning-bell, chiming pure and rich as ever.

2.5 This is Karen's day

Karen is a little knot. Tightly knit. I often pass her on my way
back and forth from the fields. She is tucked up on the doorstep
of the farmhouse, bending forwards, close to becoming a circle,
gnawing at the back of her right hand. As her body, so also her
face. Often in a grotesque grimace. Most often sad, but with a shy
hello, even a smile, on rare occasions.

She lives in a house close to ours. But her "house-parents" are
away, so this week-end she lives with us.

Last night's gathering ended with a big bang. We were all in the
living room discussing possible re-designing of the room. Discussions contain possibilities for conflicts. Karen left the field.

So also the next morning. House-duties were carried out on the
first floor. On the second floor a guest of mine was rhythmically
typing away on a manuscript. All was peace and industriousness
until new big bangs shattered the house. Karen was absolutely
wild. She ran from door to door and made a maximum of noise.
The house received a lot of punishment. Her hand was stiff, as
was her body. It was unclear whether she liked or disliked my
holding it. Slowly her hand loosened up – slightly. We, or rather
I, talked about all sorts of little things: small birds preparing for
winter out in the pinetree, people in the house, plans for the day.

At last came the question, to the source of it all: "Who is so
angry up there, who is stamping on the floor?" – the hand
tightened anew – "Who is stamping so violently above my head?"
Who?

Tuning in to Karen's fears, I could also hear it. I could hear my guest's typewriter, a distant thunder through the wooden house, a sign of creation to me, a warning signal of the utmost danger to Karen.

I gave her my interpretation, and it was all over.

2.6 The runner

Most people in the Village are a bit slow when it comes to physical movements. It is not often you see a person running or moving around quickly. Children run, but the general tendency for adults is to "skride" – which is Norwegian for a sort of solemn walk. The reasons are probably two. Villages are thoughtful places, and it is not so easy to combine thinking and running. In addition, many villagers are a bit slow physically, often also physically handicapped. They set the pace. It is as it ought to be.

Z was an exception. A few days after arrival he had been all over the place. He knew every corner, most houses, also from within, most people, but these not so much from within. He was on the move, continuously.

To the children of those living in the village he was a gift from heaven, as they were to him. At last a fast runner, a grown-up man with speed (he was 23 years, but told me once he felt like 13), a fantasy figure from outside, a playmate and not a playmate. After his arrival he was engaged in frenetic play with a group of small children, one huge bunch on the lawn.

Instinctively we intervened. The kids got too hectic, Z also. We told the kids to keep away and let Z get some rest and peace. And we told Z that he had to draw the line. He was after all a grown-up, and had also to relate to grown-ups. But it was close to impossible. The kids hunted him, and he them. Only through harsh commands were they separable.

A few days later we got to know that he had just been charged with criminal indecency with children. He was awaiting trial in the nearby prison. A social worker thought Vidaråsen might be a more suitable place.

He could not go home to his local community. Norway was in the middle of a moral panic. A small girl had been sexually abused and killed. The offender had also earlier committed acts of indecency. All over the country panic raged. All over, and of course also at Vidaråsen. Therefore it might have surprised Z that he was invited to dinner by one of the mothers shortly after arrival. The night before he had been found hiding behind a cupboard in her children's bedroom. The mother's dry comment was that she too, and not only the children, ought to get to know the new villager.

We decided to restrict his evening movements. Against strong protests, bordering on mutiny, we forced him to remain in the house during evenings, or accept our company if he had to go somewhere. It worked for four days or rather nights. The fifth night he was caught in the cafeteria opening the cash register.

The next day was his birthday. He had been promised that he could go home for a visit. His mother had baked a cake. His grandparents were to pay a visit. We drove him to the prison, claiming that both he and we had a need for time to think. He literally shrank when we told him. And so did we. He had been admitted to the village as an alternative to prison; he was the only one with that status. This made it possible to return him to prison. Two weeks later, he was admitted back into the village.

Recently his pace has slowed down. Two interpretations come to mind: we have broken him in, tamed him, converted him into one of these dull, slow grown-ups. The other interpretation is that he does not need to run any more. He has converted into a man.

It so happens that Z is good with his hands – good at repairing broken bicycles. It also so happens that the village has dozens of broken bicycles. Z works his magic. We watch him. Bikes are converted from wrecks to vehicles. Z does not have his good old reasons for running about like an animal in a cage any more. People so often stop him and ask for his advice.

This does not mean that life is easy for Z – or with him. He is not exactly a likeable person; most often provocatively dirty, hanging over the table rather than sitting in his chair, close to mute during meals, pointing at dishes he wants rather than asking for them.

True, and untrue.

Slowly his face takes on new qualities. His proud little smile when he has put cheese on his sandwich. He knows that some of us have the firm belief that the body needs some building material in addition to sugar and jam and syrup. His thrill at listening to Michael Ende's *The never ending story* (1984).

My estimate when he arrived was that Z would last four days in the village. Now he has lasted five weeks. This week-end he is with his parents. Good – and bad. It is a relief not to have to handle the continuous row of little dramas he stages around here. But at the same time, it feels unreal – a lack of challenge. A spoonful of Z a day keeps unrealities away.

Postscript; it lasted several months. His interests endured, he dared to approach girls, grown-ups. But soon he got too confident, got involved with too many girls at the same time. Some persons also found out about his former life. A move to another village rescued him. He became a highly reliable helper on a farm – until several of the surrounding summer houses were raided. Now he is in prison. There are limits to what the villages are willing and able to cope with. But we hope a third village will receive him on release.

2.7 Those who seem to cope

A great number of the village people would be in severe, definite trouble outside the village. They are different, maybe not able to read, to talk, or to earn money. For them the alternative to village life would often have been some sort of institution for some sort of handicap, or a life in extraordinary isolation. For life.

But the majority of those living in villages seem to be of another sort. The guarded formulation "seem to be" is chosen with care. Most have been able to cope before they came to the village. They cope with ordinary life after leaving, the few who leave. They cope, as most people cope. But what does it mean to cope with ordinary life? Has it something to do with not being institutionalized? Or with the level of satisfaction in that life, with a feeling of realization of oneself, a feeling of a life with purpose, of knowledge that this was a life as life ought to be?

Most have been able to cope before village life. But some have had great troubles. Some have had turbulent careers – restless travels, externally as well as internally. Some have used drugs, some have been hurt by tragic circumstances.

Foreigners are strongly represented in the villages. They are most often young. A year or two abroad, to find oneself. Often they know of these types of villages from their home-country. But several have come to stay. Often they have grown up in villages abroad. For life in the village it is a good thing that so many are from abroad. They do not have so much of an external social network. Their social energy is channelled inwards, into the village. When they explore the surroundings, they will to a large extent do it together with other people living in the village. They will have a joint handicap.

I have often brought friends to the villages, or sometimes groups of students. Usually I do not tell them beforehand whom they are going to meet. It is better just to let people meet, being received by the villagers, spread out all over the place, having meals in the individual homes and talks over coffee.

Afterwards come the questions, inevitably: Who was who? That girl in yellow, the tall man, the silent one? Behind these questions is most often a wish to know who were the normal, or more important, who were the abnormal.

Far back in time I was a willing accomplice. I answered. Conscientiously I tried to line up the villagers, create categories, explain who were mentally retarded, or insane, or just strange, or maybe extraordinarily normal. But as years have passed, the interest in this approach has faded. Knowing humans from all sorts of life situations makes it increasingly difficult to place them in simple categories. Persons we only know to a limited extent can easily be classified as mad, retarded, drug users or criminals, and administrative needs often force such categories on other people. This is one of the costs in social distance, and in institutions. But the more we come to know other people in all sorts of situations, the more unsuitable the simple categories become. A boy in the block might be given the label "delinquent", but not my own boy. I just know too much about him, his history, his generosity, his short temper, his unrealistic optimism – in combination they might make him "borrow" without asking, exactly what the law calls theft. He might have stolen, but he is not a thief to those of us who know him well. The simple categories convert into small lock-ups. Square, rigid, and not quite right for anybody. The more we know a person, the less useful these categories become. The more dangerous they also become. Categories stick. The person, influenced by his surroundings, might take on the part assigned to him and become what the label says he is.

This insight is reflected in the constitution of the villages. Here it is stated:

The purpose of the villages is to create social forms which care for the individuals as well as for the community. Here live people with different abilities as well as handicaps. All sorts of people, with all sorts of distinctive characters, are to be given opportunities to participate in this common life. The terms "patients' and "treatment personnel" are not relevant.

So, it is in harmony both with the constitution of the villages and with experience gained through living there, that this chapter does not contain an account of categories and numbers of each sort.

Nonetheless, some of the same distinctions force their way into the villages, but always with a built-in resistance. The one distinction mostly in use is *villager* versus *co-worker*. Villagers, that is mostly those who would not be able to cope alone. Most have some sort of allowance from the state. Co-workers are those who are supposed to be able to cope. Another distinction is between those with and those without a bank account. According to law, people with disability benefits have to have some portion of those benefits reserved for their own private consumption. So they all have some money in the bank, while the co-workers do not necessarily have any private money.

But these distinctions are unclear, illogical, and a constant source of frustration and confusion. All those living in the villages are villagers, independently of their ability to live outside. And all are co-workers. If anything, ideas in the village societies emphasize similarities in status and function, not dissimilarities.

Unclear distinctions, and illogical, but difficult to avoid as long as the villages operate in a society of our type. Cars are to be run. Not everybody is able to. Telephones are to be used. Again, there are some who cannot. Money is exchanged. Some do it with greater ease than others. Some are to stuff dolls with wool for months in a row, some comb the cows, some chime the bell, some write the letters. The villages invest much energy in keeping the technology on a level suitable for most people. But it is impossible to do away with all complexities. Thereby the demands valid in the general society are transplanted into the village society. Independently of ideas about equality, some basic differences press forward. A tendency to thinking in categories reappears. We get the villager- co-worker distinction. Or those with or without a bank account. First come the conditions, then concepts follow. These village communities have, however, less of these distinctions than any other existing social system I know of, and the differences decrease with length of stay in the village. The often expressed ideal is to become a villager. That all become villagers.

By saying that these villages are constructed in such a way that the usual diagnostic categories break down, and furthermore that this is also a conscious wish expressed in the constitution, we have actually taken a first step towards a more general understanding of what sort of phenomena these villages represent. We are given the first possibilities of placing them on the sociological world atlas.

In this atlas there are two continents. The one consists of people in relation to each other. It has to do with social life, interdependence, communes, societies. It also often has to do with shades rather than contrasts, changes rather than stability, and with ambiguity and doubt. This continent is one badly suited for counting and statistics.

The other continent in the sociological world atlas consists of categories rather than groups, and with clarity and accountability as major virtues. It is thus a continent suited for statistics. But statistics are not only a counting system. They are also a thought system. They presuppose a certain way of thinking and also influence thinking. Statistical activities do not only describe what already exists, but contribute actively to the creating of new phenomena. To be able to count, the phenomena have to be ordered in categories divided from all other phenomena. When ordered in such categories, they are also ordered in ways suited for large scale organizations like institutions or even States (Østerberg 1987, pp. 87–96 and 1988, pp. 18–44).

But this whole chapter has described life on the other social continent. We have described a system with humans who are *not* easy to classify and where there is a will not to make it easy. Many *change continuously*. And they are seen as *similar in attributes* where professionals, usual organizations and government are accustomed to finding the most important differences. As a first characteristic of the villages we might therefore conclude: The villages encourage social life of a type that offers exceptionally strong resistance against being shaped in categories suitable for the counting system of the State, that is for statistics. In the spirit of Foucault (1977) these villages can be seen as small nests of opposition against the hegemony of State categorization.

3

Home

Five villages. Different landscapes, different climates, different people; five villages implanted in highly different local cultures. Nonetheless similar. If you have been in one, you have been in all. This is not completely true, as each village has its own style, its own trademark, its own pride. But still. You come from one village to the next. You open the door. You are home.

There are many reasons for this similarity and they will, I hope, unfold as the pages pass. First and foremost the similarity is caused by the fact that so many extraordinary people exist in these houses. In addition come some basic principles of village life, principles stronger than local culture and differences in people, climates and landscapes. It has to do with style of home-life, style of working-life, and style of cultural life. And it has to do with a non-relationship to money. But let us start at home.

3.1 Shared living

Idiots, mad and bad. That would be the folk characteristics of a large portion of those living in the villages. In addition there are some other people who just prefer to live in villages. Maybe they are, by and large, just ordinary or maybe not. Maybe we have not found out yet about their peculiarities. In any case, these villages are places with the most extreme variations. Some come to the village with a history of having been locked up for years in small rooms as dangerous. Some come there out of an urge to find a meaning in life. Some of them find it. Some hate it all and leave at the first opportunity.

But if they stay, they will all live in a household where most sorts of people are represented. This is the basic principle of these villages: *no segregation according to "ability" or "normality"*. In each household ordinary as well as not so ordinary people are living together. Most have separate rooms, but there is no separate wing for people with peculiar habits. Some people who need to be protected against noise might be given rooms on the periphery of the houses. That is as far as segregation goes.

The same principle applies to the use of all common rooms. They are for all. And it applies to the most important of domestic activities: the meals. One big table, with all the people in the house mixed around it.

The house-mother or house-father most often sits at the top of the table, seeing to it that all get what they need. Small children most often sit close to their parents. Some parents make exceptions for some meals and have them with their children in private rooms. Small children might need special attention; the table becomes too big. Some senior people take their breakfast alone – a protection against an overwhelming amount of social life. But these are rare exceptions. The usual arrangement is the big table, the complete mixture, and a conversation between all. Sometimes the conversation takes place between two or three people, maybe on a topic that others are not able to follow. In some houses this is close to usual. But as in social life in general, seclusive behaviour in the midst of the common room is seen as impolite and therefore frowned on. The norm is one of general participation.

Every house has one person who is particularly responsible for that house. Nearly always this is a person without a pension, the mark of being disabled. But here too there are exceptions. Some clearly disabled persons have the major responsibility within some houses. Those responsible are called "house-mother" or "house-father". Some live in couples and/or have children of their own.

After breakfast, all – except the house-father or the house-mother – leave for work somewhere else. Sometimes the house-father or mother also leaves, at least for half a day. But some other people come from other houses. Housework – cleaning and cooking – is defined as work and is carried out by someone from another house. It is seen as important to have a split between place of work and place of living.

Around midday the house is full again, and in the evening before the onset of cultural activities. Saturday afternoon and Sundays are also days of great activity in the houses.

This may sound peaceful, as a harmonious way of organizing

daily life, well arranged, predictable, but it is not. Let me describe a day in a house, seen from the perspective of an ordinary co-worker on an ordinary Saturday. The only exceptional feature of the situation was that there was no house-father or mother at home that day. Let me describe life:

   . . . when A is sick from the very early morning, complaining of pain in the stomach,
   . . . when B does not clean his room, nor the stairs,
   . . . when C is to prepare for the Bible evening, but spends her time in B's room
   . . . when D decides to take over some of the cleaning of the stairs for B, but does not get the vacuum-cleaner to operate because B to prove his strength has tightened the tubes too firmly together. And I am not strong enough either.
   . . . When A is worse, complaining heavily, maybe he will die, and I do not remember the name of the nurse, nor her house.
   . . . By good luck a co-worker drops in and tells me the name, but now the telephone is out of function and the alternative telephone has disappeared
   . . . and A is complaining even more and C who is out of B's room, appears and ask me to control the time for the eggs she is about to boil, and I put B into action, but the nurse has arrived and orders ca-momile tea, and we have no such tea in the house and I ask E to run over to the neighbours to borrow some, but E who cannot read, insists that we have camomile tea and to prove that it is not necessary for him to run over to the neighbours, drags me through 20 boxes of tea that I have looked through before until I run myself and get the tea but for-get the eggs that are boiling, so C gets absolutely mad at me
   . . . until
the nurse comes down from A and says that he is just one big smile. All he needed was some extra attention
   and the eggs did not turn out too bad after all, so I am forgiven
   and D managed the vacuum-cleaner and is just happy to have cleaned the stairs
   and B has actually cleaned his room
   and when I come to think of it, I have heard that C can't have chil-dren, so I don't have to trouble my mind about the possibly very con-crete consequences of a romance which probably was not much more than sharing some chocolate
   and when I visit A he is still just one big smile and is more than strong enough to push me down into his chair, holding of my hands in a very firm grasp, and placing the other one on his forehead
   . . . one more of those ordinary days in the village.

3.2 Not a drop spilt[1]

Most people around the tables in these houses are supposed to be
dumb. I was thinking of that one day during an evening meal
years ago when I was a newcomer to one of the villages. We were
probably ten people around the table. Vidar asked if we wanted
more tea, and served us all, quietly, no mess, not a drop spilt. In
addition to being designated mentally deficient, Vidar is blind.
But the point of the story is not that the blind, classified as mentally deficient, Vidar, served tea. The point is the behaviour of the
remaining persons around the table. It was a matter of course that
Vidar should serve tea. It was an atmosphere of confidence. I
think I observed a slightly watchful glance on the face of one who
had taken particular responsibility in setting the table, but no in-
terference, no comments afterwards. This was not the result of
planning. I asked an old acquaintance the next day. He insisted;
no strategy, it had never been discussed in the household.

The only threat I can envisage against the circle of people
around that table, is that there might be too many helpers about.
Not professionals, they are in the daily life largely banned from
this community, at least in their capacity as professionals. But do-
gooders. It is a very realistic threat. Young people are attracted to
this community. They queue up to take part for parts of their life.
Too many would easily think that they should take the teapot
away from Vidar and maybe even push him out of his major job
in the household: drying the dishes. He does it, once a day, in addition to his other job outside the household. To protect Vidar
and others, dishwashers are not allowed into the system. Also to
protect him, some of the young people who would otherwise be
tempted to give too much help are forced to take their meals in a
ghetto where there are none of the formerly declared mentally de-
ficients, no insane, no blind, no crippled. In other words the situation has been turned exactly upside down. The youngsters have
become the handicapped, those to protect the others against.

And the young people know it. They strive to get access, to get
close to a totality, to get teachers of all sorts, that is, from the
whole variety of mankind, in vital questions.

This is a continuous struggle. At least three times Vidaråsen has
made attempts to create segregated houses, that is, houses where

1 I have described this episode in my book *Limits to Pain* (1981).

only young and supposedly not handicappéd people live, or short-time visitors from the ordinary society live, or where ordinary people in need of rest might get some peace. But it does not work. Young people become even younger left to themselves. Short-time visitors did not come to remain alone. People in need of rest start to wonder what rest really means. Is it the absence of sounds and smiles? Even tears? One experience from village life is this: A household turns sour if the variance of those living there becomes too narrow. And people get sour, preoccupied with their own problems and private miseries.

3.3 Important – but not all-important

Home life in the villages is probably of less total importance than usual in north-western Europe. Common rooms are less elaborate. Furniture is a bit below the usual Scandinavian standard and some of the small symbols of privacy are not as abundantly represented as usual. The number of things are more at the level earlier found in southern countries, and some of the reasons are probably the same. In the south of Europe, at least until recently, more time was spent on public ground. Climate, material resources, and social organization made this natural. In Vidaråsen and the other villages an abundance of public buildings compensates for the climatic handicaps of the north, a negative attitude towards consumerism sets limits to the excessive amount of things in the rooms, and at the same time the social organization also tempts people out of the homes. In addition comes the diminished importance of freedom of privacy so often associated with the shielded life behind the walls of the home.

3.4 On solitude

To exist in one of these homes in the villages, and to enjoy it raises the question of the criteria for good home-life. Is home a place for recharging batteries, a castle for re-creation, or maybe a place for creation? Is home the goal, or parts of the process? And what about the privileges of being alone, digesting impressions from life in other arenas, licking one's wounds, recovering?

The need for solitude is often expressed by visitors to the village: "How do you manage to be with people all the time, not to be left alone, not to be free to remain only in your own company?"

Maybe the explanation has to do with the relative absence of pretence.

A great number of those living in these types of villages are not particularly efficient in hiding who they are and what they think. By this they create an honesty-level above the usual. In addition comes the social organization. As will be developed in later chapters, these villages are of a type where all are continuously exposed to each other in most areas of social life. They know each other from home-life through work and into culture and leisure. The totality of what is presented to the others within the village is the result of endless numbers of joint encounters in all sorts of life situations. This represents a drive for consistency. It leaves little room for role players only known within one particular sector and with a hidden life in other sectors. Instead we meet personalities, characters – people with a consistent behaviour wherever they appear. In this situation home-life gets another quality. Behind the quest for "My home is my castle" and the shielded life with solitude as the extreme example, there is probably a reality of life outside the home in the form of a life with pretences. Home becomes the place to remove the veil, to be oneself, completely. Solitude creates space and time to reconcile the public picture to the private. But then, if village life because of the type of people and the type of organization is a life with a minimum of veils to be worn, then it is also possible to understand why solitude is not seen to be of overriding importance. Most is known. There is not so much to hide. It is therefore easier to be oneself in the midst of the others. It is possible to experience in the company of others the freedom usually associated with solitude .

This interpretation may give more meaning to another experience: It has so happened in my life that I have spent much time with several sorts of extraordinary people, particularly those called mentally retarded, but also a with considerable number of people called mad or extraordinarily bad. Over time I find an increased preference for just that sort of company. And I know I am not alone in this. Humans supposed to be retarded, to be mad, to be extraordinarily bad, have something in common. Not deviance, but consistency. They are – more than usual people – above, or below, pretences. Borderline people might be just the opposite.

They struggle to pass as normal. But those solidly on the wrong side have an authenticity which is of exceptional attraction.

Nora dropped in the week after she had so vividly taken part in a seminar on mental institutions. She obviously had rich experiences from such places, vulnerable to the extreme. She turned the seminar upside down; chaos reigned for a while. The day after the seminar she went back to the hospital for a short rest, then out again without pretence, without armour, allowing me too to do away with pretences. Such visitors create a sort of peace in the office, a peace that remains in the walls.

True, and untrue. I do not know Nora. I never will. I do not know those living in the villages, and of course not myself. Maybe it has to do with respect. Living in these villages gives extraordinary room for *accepting people as they are*. This includes tolerance for *not* knowing all about each other. The need for solitude is reduced in situations where there is little demand to be as all others. Exceptional people create space around themselves, as well as around those who get to know them. The Camphill villages are social systems particularly suited to help that process. They create space for closeness, for solitude without loneliness.

3.5 Love life

In the first edition of the manuscript this section was not included. This was forcefully brought to my attention by critical colleagues: Reading your manuscript, it sounds as if life in the homes is a life without secrets. Particularly it sounds as if sex-life does not exist. Have urges for love and sensual pleasures disappeared in the villages, what goes on in these homes?

My omission is in itself a finding. It is a reflection of the fact that the villages are relatively usual places to live in. There is less pretence there than in many other places, but there is also privacy and shyness. It does not feel natural to make inquiries about the love life of those living in the village. Therefore I do not know much about sex life in the villages, just as I do not know much about sex-life among my neighbours or friends in Oslo. The villages are not institutions. There are limits to visibility and no accounting system as so often found in institutions. People fall in love. Some, but not many, move together. Some are more discreetly living together. I suppose many of those living single enjoy sex through masturbation. I have not asked. Nor have I asked my neighbours in Oslo. Some have unstable relationships in Vidaråsen, as elsewhere. Some break common norms in a visible way or create so much conflict that their behaviour is met with common disapproval. Several of those living in the village are rather slow in realizing wishes. This might be one reason for the lack of known pregnancies among those supposed to be handicapped there. But several use contraceptives. In Oslo more than half of all females will once in their life have gone through an abortion. I do not know those among my neighbours who have, and those who have not. I do not feel free to ask. Nor do I feel free to ask at Vidaråsen. It would be beneath one's dignity. Mine and theirs.

But public rooms are free for all. It was there I saw Gudrun, the new Gudrun. Just a short glimpse, passing behind some columns. She was so new, I was not sure, could it be her, but then another look, and right, it was Gudrun.

She was the first villager who came to Vidaråsen. Her brother was one of the founders, to help her. She liked it there, but life was far from perfect. She was good at washing floors, but all took place in some sort of anger. Mumbling, noisy, a face in thousands of wrinkles, close to a witch in appearance, an aura of unrest.

This was Gudrun, until that day behind the column. A complete change. A peace beyond comprehension. A face radiant with joy. Gudrun and Johannes. It had just happened, at a joint meeting of two villages. Johannes was from the other village. A big, but rather slow man. He packed his suitcase the week after they had met and moved to Gudrun's village. The next year they exchanged rings in an airplane just passing the Alps, like a story in a weekly, but with a more realistic end; now they live side by side in two rooms, spending much time together, but also a considerable part of that time in rather noisy conflicts. I do not know the character of their intimate life and would not dream of asking, but I share the joy in the fact that they met, and the common concern that the relationship might break down.

4

Work

4.1 Dangerous tools

Rare species are always in danger of extinction. Villages in a modern world are in particular danger. They are few and far between. They are on several counts in severe contrast to the dominant culture. They are dependent on a great amount of reflections and self-insight to be able to protect themselves against what is "obvious" in the external world. Let me illustrate this by telling the story of three types of tools. These tools are taken for granted in most parts of the industrialized world. For the villagers they represent great problems. First, a story of defeat:

The local telephone

Once upon a time Vidaråsen had two postmen. They were important persons with a special cap and a sack for the mail. Their pride was great. With dignity they delivered mail from the central box to each house. In addition they delivered the internal mail. A stream of messages was dependent on their reliability. Without them the village was in trouble.

Today they are not quite the same persons, or rather, not the same creators of a work. Half their task is gone, taken by the telephone. An internal telephone system has been created. Plans for this were mentioned at a meeting of the board of directors. Strong protests were raised. Nonetheless, some years later, and without having passed the board, the telephones were in and parts of the job out.

Again strong protests. For a period the protestors were able to ban one version of the newest system from being put into use. It was installed, but not switched on. But in vain. As this book goes to press, a brand new streamlined system is available. A system so complicated that the first manual of instruction missed a basic point. This united everybody in a joint feeling of impatience. A new manual has corrected this and will give a selected few a tool of communication. The social consequences are threefold: Jobs lost. Creation of situations which underline the difference between them and us. And also important: Local telephone means a certain reduction in the number of people out on roads and tracks. Instead of a small trip to the neighbours with a message, the telephone is used. Convenient, and as we shall see later, socially dangerous.

Dishwashers

A twenty years' war has raged over dishwashers. Hygienic matters have top priority within health institutions. Initially the villages were defined as belonging to the Ministry of Health, they were doctors' and nurses' territory. Health personnel fight germs. Dishwashers are good germ-killers.

But they also kill work. Work of a type well suited for many persons in the villages, and also well suited for social life around the sink. But it is difficult work. It has to be admitted that all dishes are not all the time up to all the standards of the Ministry of Health. When health inspectors arrive, alarms are sounded in the villages. The local telephone becomes of real use, forks and kettles are given hurried attention, but excessive quotas of germs are still registered.

The general view in the village is that sterile surroundings are probably dangerous, but some compromises have been accepted. Cafeterias in the villages are places where particularly many guests are served. Guests are unaccustomed to the local breed of bacteria. Here dishwashers are accepted. But not in the houses.

Farm equipment

Farms in the villages are run according to biodynamic principles. Basically this means that one tries to make nature into an ally, not a potential enemy. Farming and gardening are not a fight against nature, but a collaborative effort. Nature has to be observed, studied, understood, and then helped to give more of what humans want. Pesticides are banned; instead one attempts to strengthen nature's own defence systems against weeds or other unwanted attacks. Artificial fertilizers are also banned; instead composts are used to the utmost. The difference between biological and biodynamic farming is that the latter also relies on certain substances supposed to be potentized as in homoeopathy, activated in a special process throughout the winter and later spread on the fields. The biodynamic growers also pay close attention to old farm calendars. The sowing ought to be carried out when the moon and stars are in the best position, and this varies between different type of seeds.

This is a book on villages as social systems, not on farming. Our questions will not be of the type; what sort of farming gives most grain or milk? Our question will be: What are the social consequences of various forms of farming?

Biological and biodynamic farming have this in common: they are good for rainworms. Rainworms are seen as an ally to keep the earth in good condition. But this has consequences for what sort of equipment one can put above the rainworms. It ought to be light equipment, otherwise the earth will become packed and the worms squeezed. And pesticides have to be banned. They kill worms as well as weeds. Light equipment often means that real horsepower is needed, as well as manpower. Lack of pesticides sometimes means that weeds get out of control, and again manpower is the only alternative. Good. Hands are needed, including hands not quite so able as most others. But also bad on a rainy day, wet, miserable. The neighbour's field looks beautifully free from weeds, a consequence of the pesticides he sprayed out last month, sitting high up on his giant tractor. Villagers also want vacations, with their families, or jointly, out of the village. The farmer, and a few of his helpers, tend to be alone during just those weeks when they are most in need of help.

Then comes the temptation. The fields could be better protected by a tractor than by horses, better still by a large tractor than a small one. The farmer is a man of honour. His fields are his honour. In addition, there is the fact that the big tractor can also more easily keep the roads free of snow during winter. So efficient is the tractor that voices are raised in favour of developing the narrow tracks into roads broad enough to be free of snow by the help of the tractor. Several villagers have trouble in walking. Several old co-workers are also in trouble. An efficient tractor could spread sand on every icy road on every icy morning long before any vulnerable person was out. In the final analysis, seen from the angle of both farmers and comfort and health inspectors, is not the health of villagers more important than rainworms?

Tractors *have* arrived in all five villages. Milking machines have not. Cows are close to humans. It is not kind towards any living subject to restrict it to the barn through the whole Nordic winter. Therefore each day the cows and the ox are let out in the snow. But kindness has its costs. Two winters ago the best milking cow at Vidaråsen fell on the ice, broke her leg and had to be slaughtered. But generally cows in the villages have happy days. Before milking they are brushed for hours. It helps to produce milk, according to the farmers' theory. At least it looks good, for the cows and for those brushing. In some villages one job during milking is the job of tail-keeper, grasping the tail firmly, to prevent the tail of the cow from going into the face of the person who is milking. But the key person is, of course, the one who milks. Not all are able, but for those who are, this activity is a source of great joy.

Tractors have arrived. But they have not been allowed to swallow up the tracks. And they are used with considerable care in the fields. All sorts of additional equipment which make hands superfluous have not been added. In particular, most of the harvesting is still done by hand. Doll shops, bakery and pottery are closed on big harvesting days; the whole village is out in the field. Some picking the carrots, some removing their green tops, some placing them in cardboard boxes, some serving tea, some just enjoying the communal existence, and some playing hookey and obstructing other people's work. I stopped Z (p. 20) from doing just that, and asked him to help me with the picking. He made some jokes and disappeared. I caught him anew, more firmly this time. He tried once more, and at last I got his point. He just was not sure what a carrot was and particularly not sure how to get one up from the earth. He, the public enemy in his local neighbourhood, was scared to death of exposing his incompetence. Rather bad than dumb, a tendency so clearly documented by Edgerton (1967).

Local telephones, farm equipment, dishwashers, – they are all dangerous tools if used without insight.

4.2 Types of work

Housework absorbs a lot of people's energy in the villages. Each morning those assigned to these tasks arrive from other houses, to clean and to cook. Except for the house-father or house-mother nobody does daily work in his or her own house. The importance of work is to do it for others. It goes on for one hour and a half, then half an hour with tea and cakes and reading aloud or chatting with the house-father or mother. Then continued work until they leave for their own dinner in their own house. Afternoons are most often spent in workshops for those who do housework in the morning.

Another important work is the making of dolls. The leader of one of these doll shops once gave a description of this work (Leinslie 1984). The quotations given here from her description are a bit long, given the format of this book. But the process she describes has also been a long one. She is very soft-spoken. But if one listens with attention, one gets lots of information:

> In the spring of 1981 a new workshop for the creation of dolls was established.
>
> One such workshop was already operating; here they made dolls for children aged four to five. Now we wanted to make one for very small children. The goal was to create a doll so that the child could recognize the experience of herself. The body and the legs are more out of consciousness for a very small child. Therefore, we made the doll with formed head and hands, while the body and legs remained as a soft sack.
>
> A workshop is a mini-community. And a community where we can feel equal. It is easy to see that all activities are important for the final product. If one link disappears, consequences follow for the whole process. But not only because of the productivity. Something in the whole atmosphere is missing when one person is not there.
>
> For each participant it is important to know that she or he is of importance for the totality. Outside the workshop Ola has lots of trouble. He is aggressive, agitated, very much awake, always on guard. But he is also kind and helpful, and cares particularly for those weaker than himself. He came from an institution where he was described as aggressive in all confrontation, and refusing all sorts of work.
>
> . . . during his first period in the workshop, he did all his sewing by hand. He could only cope with the simplest of tasks, restless, not engaged in what he did. He used to transport material around in the village, to get an outlet for his restlessness. Slowly, however, he proved able to operate a sewing machine. It all started with the simplest possible lines, then gradually complications increased. He managed. Today he prepares all the sewing processes, makes drawings according to a pattern, cuts the material, and sews. The work is carried out with

extreme precision and care. The tool has become a blessing for him. To master this machinery and having a work which is his own has meant a lot. He knows what to do, and also what is waiting the next day. It puts an end to his restlessness. He is now present in his own work. He has become an inspirator in the workshop.

In the house she lives in, Aud is a quiet person. Days can pass without a word from her. She has her habits in the house, and can't be moved an inch if not in the right mood. Also in the workshop this might happen. But only seldom now. She has got a special type of contact with Ola and is thereafter more happy. She becomes flexible, generous. Sometimes she helps Thor, threads his needle, so that he can do the rest himself. When Helen arrived in the workshop, she cared for her from the first day. She accompanies her back and forth between the workshop and Helen's house every day.

Aud sews by hand on the dolls. They are close to finished when she gives them away. She sees a person with life in the dolls, often she hugs them. She likes to have several dolls at her desk, and says that she is to sew on them all. When ready, she says "here you get a gift from me". She gives from herself. Her joy over work spreads out to the others.

It is as if the villagers come out of themselves in the workshops. There are not so many disturbing elements there, and there is all the time a repetition in what happens. It creates an atmosphere where they dare to open up. It gives opportunities to give, both in production and in the process of human interaction.

Most other workshops in the Villages are like the one for dolls. Not always so systematically thought through, and often populated with persons with less severe physical and mental problems. There are a pottery, a carpenter's shop, a weaving workshop, a small cement factory, several greenhouses, the farm, and a bakery. Tom is the pillar here. A year ago he took his certificate as a "bakersvenn", that is a fully qualified baker. His diploma-work was "wienerbrød" for the whole Village. He is probably the first person in Norway with Down's syndrome (in folk-language: mongoloid) who has qualified as a journeyman. For those close to him this was no great surprise. His will power is exceptional. So also is his inventiveness. Bread and cakes are best from ovens preheated by real wood. Vidaråsen has one that needs to be lit at four o'clock in the morning. Tom has done it for years. A while ago his alarm-clock broke down. He did not tell anybody, but solved the problem by gulping down three big glasses of water just before he went to bed. Then nature aroused him at around four.

4.3 Work or labour?

The inevitable question is probably: How are they paid? And the simple answer is: They are not. Nobody in the Villages is paid, neither those with certified disorders, nor the others. People just work. To a large extent with enthusiasm. Some with a pronounced ability to take it easy. But money, or its absence, is not a part of motivation for work. I cannot remember any discussion in the villages concerning payment for work. Money is discussed. How much money it is right to use. Or how much the dolls ought to cost in the shop. But not money as an incentive for work. Work and money are unrelated matters. This is of great consequence for the meaning of work in the village. To understand more, let us turn to the older meaning of the words:

Labour is traditionally used for heavy, strenuous, uninspired activity. Often it hurts. The dictionaries tell us that labour imposes strains on body and soul, particularly if it is enforced. Prisons are filled with exemplifications. The tread-mill is described in detail and with enthusiasm in old literature from the prisons. It was the ideal labour. Large groups of humans were forced to walk upstairs. Side by side they trod on huge planks that sank under the weight of the human bodies. If they did not walk fast enough, they sank themselves. Often the mill milled. Sometimes it only moved. Anyhow, the arrangement created great tranquillity in the institution.

Work is a brighter prospect. Far back is a connection with the terms "Virke" or "Verk". *Verk* might be an accomplished piece of art. "Virke" is activity leading to a piece of "verk".

The Villages have a constitution. The essence of that constitution is that everybody should work for the benefit of others. As nurses do, when they comfort. Or as artists do, when they create for an audience. Nobody should work for themselves. That is the way of creating a sound social system, insisted Rudolf Steiner, who formulated this constitution. We might add: When money is used as an incentive, an activity will often be transformed from work to labour. An act loses its character of work – "verk, virke" – when payment becomes the incentive. Thus the central question becomes; what sorts of acts in what circumstances are given the meaning of being work rather than labour?

Most children work most of the time; they are actively creating, putting dolls to bed, building hideouts, creating alliances for combat. Then comes, in our types of systems and for many of them: labour. Seen from several perspectives, the essential task would be to preserve the quality of work in most acts carried out. The task would be to preserve us as life-long creators. A dissolution of the seemingly "obvious' association between monetary rewards and tasks needed to be done would probably do more to preserve creators than any other political act. Minimum wages for all – independent of any contribution they were able to offer – might in this perspective become a crucial act. If a minimum of money was available to all – which is no unrealistic economic option in the west – more people might continue to act as children, like artists, like those who build cathedrals for reasons other than economic ones. Useless tasks would be rehabilitated. We would be one step back in the right direction, towards a world with unlimited opportunities for work. With a dissolution of the connection between task and reward, we might also undermine some wage-earners' feeling that their consumption is "deserved". "Deserved" because it is earned through their own effort. We would then be more able to initiate a constructive debate on alternative criteria for suitable consumption. In the villages this leads to a general attitude of austerity.

I had a problem during my stay at Vidaråsen. The work I was assigned, was time-consuming, but not a heavy task. Energy built up. I tried to get rid of it by some jogging around the pathways. It was impossible. Everywhere I met people. I could not just pass them, running. Encounters are for talks. Or worse: Those I met were at work. If I had nothing else to do than just idle running, why not give them a hand? I tried to be out before dawn, but H. was out picking onions together with one of his two girl-friends. They should not have been there until after breakfast. Also the farmer was out. The baker as well. Evenings were filled with culture and people on all tracks. Nights had to be reserved for sleep. I packed my pair of jogging-shoes away. They belonged to another life.

4.4 All the money in one hat

Some people have fantasies about the villages as self-supporting systems. This is nothing more than just that – fantasies. How could villages, with such a great quota of atypical members, be able to accomplish what ordinary farms cannot do without great state subsidies, and what ordinary institutions cannot do without close to total public coverage of all costs? The villages have model functions. If the state economy goes to pieces, if a national catastrophe threatens, they might be better off than most arrangements. But today they are close to being totally dependent on resources from the outside. The interesting aspect of their economy is not the input, but how they use these resources.

But first, for the record, on input: The money which streams into the villages, comes from the State, from the counties, from private sources and from production in the villages. Our figures are from Vidaråsen, but the other villages are basically similar. Most comes from the State, last year 21 million kroner (2 million pounds). Close to an additional million kroner comes from the counties. From the farms and from the shops also comes a considerable amount of money – close to 10 per cent of the total income. Private money has mostly been provided through actions carried out by last year's pupils in the *gymnas* (secondary school). In the spring term they spend one day for a purpose they like. They like the villages. They have often sold candles, produced in the villages. Many houses in the villages have been built through this money. Private support is a controversial solution in a welfare-state. Should not people in need of help receive it fully through the State? Are not private contributions a degrading heritage from older times with private charity? The argument against this view is that thousands of young people each year learn about the villages and also spread this information to the buyers of the candles. Some of these young people end up as residents in the villages.

Then to the use of the money. Here comes the basic principle of all the money in one hat. The public money for the villages is given as if the villages were public institutions. In the budget are titles such as "teacher", "nurse", "qualified nurse", "doctor" etc. These concepts are without meaning in the villages. Therefore the money officially granted for these official roles is put into a joint account. The official job holders never see the money.

But she or he is cared for and given a room in the house, food, a car if necessary, or a train-ticket. And at present for the younger participants some 700 kroner a month. It simplifies the accounting system. They are for flowers or books or personal gifts. But he or she might need more. Then comes the money from the hat: a vacation in Greece. Or a seminar in Järna. Or one in Moscow. Or a new dress. The hat with money is there at the disposal of all co-workers. Senior people might receive less than the 700 kroner each month. The danger in the system is certainly not abuse in the sense of taking out too much for personal use. It is under-consumption that is the problem – a hesitation to use, a celebration of austerity creating hardships in the daily life. Ideally people should watch each other and encourage friends to renew outworn commodities. But all is not visible, and humans are often shy in these matters.

The reaction from people outside the villages is often simply disbelief. It is not possible. It will lead to abuse. But try to talk to very old people. So old that they do not talk about the "State health system", but about "Sykekasse" – the little box they all put their share into during weeks when they were lucky enough not to be unemployed – the box they relied on if the body failed. This money was also the comrade's money. The situation was exactly the same as with the money in the hat. An experience of common destiny made under consumption much more probable than over-consumption. Level of consumption is a direct consequence of the organization of the social system.

The consequences of money in the hat are three-fold. First, as already described, it cuts the relationship between work and money. Work is protected against becoming labour. Persons can be evaluated – and evaluate themselves – according to what they do and how they do it, not according to what sort of money it brings. Secondly, it also severs the relationship between work and consumption. Money is not deserved through work. Thirdly, shared money in a hat does also make the village as a unit much more powerful. Collective living is cheap living – as long as austerity is the ideal and the collectives do not grow too large. In addition there is the fact that everybody living in the village is taxed according to his or her actual consumption, not their formal income. They pay taxes from their 700 kroner a month, plus an amount for house and food which they receive in the village plus what they get for eventual extra private use.

According to the original estimates behind the budget, Vidaråsen receives salaries from the State for 30 paid workers. According to the State, these are the employees. But in reality there are about 45 such workers with salaries in the villages. In other words: 15 extra people are paid out of the surplus in the hat. The same is the case in the other villages.

From this hat comes in addition money for a continuous expansion of the villages. New villages are bought from the money in the hat. And new buildings are supported from the same source. In 1987 one million Kroner were put aside for such purposes. Nearly all of it was surplus from the hat.

There are three exceptions to this basic principle for village economy. The most important one has already been mentioned. All people with disabilities that entitle them to state pensions are to have a portion of this pension reserved for their own private consumption. They have their own bank account. At present (1988) they get 750 Kroner each month. They will most often have more in pocket money than those who could be called employed take out in salaries.

The other exception is that some people might have some personal belongings or money from life outside or before the village life. It is up to them to keep it. One pensioned co-worker at Vidaråsen has his own car.

A third exception: Some villages might hire some people who live outside the village. Vidaråsen has had both a bus driver, an EDP-expert, and a typist from a nearby town. Jøssåsen relies on a car driver and a weaver from outside. But nobody living inside the village receives for personal use an ordinary salary for his or her work.

The daily cost for those officially cared for within Vidaråsen in 1989 is NOK 550. A few years earlier the figure was NOK 450. This last figure can be compared with other figures. Here are some:

	Norwegian Kroner (NOK)
Average costs per patient per day in institutions for the mentally handicapped in Norway	992.–
Average costs per patient in somatic hospitals 1985	2,000.–
Average costs per patient in psychiatric hospitals 1985	1,300.–
Average costs per prisoner 1987	726.–
Average costs in Crisis Centres for females (food not included)	215.–

As we see, villages are inexpensive even compared to institutions for the mentally handicapped. They are cheap indeed when compared to hospitals and prisons. And if we for a moment should stick to the terminology of the official society, they are extremely inexpensive when we consider that a much higher number of persons are "employed" than those "paid" for by the officials, and when we consider all the "extra" buildings – theatre halls, cafeterias, workshops – that are built on the basis of these NOK 550 per day. Salaries are the major expense in all institutions. Normally they are used for private consumption or invested outside the system. In the villages salaries are mostly invested in the system for the benefit of the totality.

5

The Rhythm

5.1 The week

Waking up in the villages is a soft process. Often someone is walking around in the house playing a flute, sometimes other instru-
ments are used. For most people this is sufficient, even though
some are in need of a more direct command. But there are incen-
tives to be ready at seven thirty. A candle is burning in the living
room, a poem is read, a song is sung, and then breakfast.

Meals have their own rhythm. Mostly all around one table, with
a benediction for the food, most often this one:

Earth who gave to us this food
Sun who made it ripe and good
Dear Earth
Dear Sun
by you we live
to you our loving
thanks we give

Then all present say "Bless the food" while they hold hands with
their neighbours around the table.

It is a foreign procedure for those coming from the outside
world. Visitors look shy. For those of us outside this belief system
it is a dilemma; how far is it possible to express blessings for unre-
cognized powers? For me, participation in rituals around meals is
not going too far. On the contrary, these mornings are good mornings. Mostly meals do not commence before everyone is there.
The candle, the holding of hands – it encourages being there in
time, and is also a unifying process. And then the common meal,
and a united "Thanks for the food". It is a welcome contrast to
the hurried meals of the outside world, so often without any common start, no core, no common end.

At twenty-five past eight a bell chimes; it is time to leave the houses. Work commences at nine. The bakery and farm are exceptions, with much earlier starts. At work the rhythm from breakfast is repeated. Coming together, maybe a song before starting, then work for an hour or two, then a break with tea, often combined with one person reading to the group a chapter from a book, and at last a joint farewell when the first part of the working-day is over at half past twelve.

What follows is the midday break. In modern Norwegian "middag" – midday – is a term used for the major meal, independently of when it is consumed. In the villages the term is brought back to its original use. There "middag" means middle of the day, and it also means the major meal. The food is hot, and the break is a long one, – also as in older times, or like the siestas of the southern countries. Time for the meal and for rest. Most often coffee and cakes are consumed jointly in the living room.

The afternoon shifts are like those of the mornings. Many continue at their morning's place of work. These shifts last from half past two until half past five. Some, particularly those who have been in housework, will now take up activities in workshops. Others move into various educational activities, lessons in reading, the orchestra has rehearsals, some are in town visiting the dentist, etc. At five the evening bell chimes, the work is over, everybody goes home for the evening meal.

But activities do not cease. Nearly every evening the villages have some sort of program, most often in the largest room or hall the village can muster. And again there is a rhythm throughout the program. Often silence before it all starts, and then some music or song at the end. Beginnings and ends are clearly marked. Smaller groups often gather in a circle with the same number of chairs as there are persons. There are no tables in between. Lecturers in big rooms often find themselves without a protective table between themselves and those who listen.

The days in the villages are like small wheels, similar to each other. Breakfast rolls along, with a united beginning and end. So do the morning work, the dinners, the afternoon work, the evening meals, and the evening activities. On a normal day of work there are six encounters, six small wheels, with a similar structure. And then six days a week with the same structure. The villages work on Saturdays. This is a conscious choice, which will soon be described.

5.2 Peak of the week

Saturday nights are different. Many co-workers, but not all, are anthroposophists. It is easier to say what this system of ideas and beliefs is not than what it is. To put it briefly, it is not an elaborate dogmatic system. It is not in disharmony with major parts of Christianity. It has services close to the usual Christian ones, but mostly not carried out by professionals. And in addition, it cherishes a belief in reincarnation and that our destinies are determined by our deeds in former lives and furthered by cultivating our new possibilities in this life though we have to do our utmost to cultivate these possibilities.

This description will not satisfy the anthrosophists, but that is not my project. What I am up to is to explain why Saturday nights in the villages are such good nights. Mostly to explain it to myself, a disbeliever.

Saturday nights are the best of all nights. Long before that night, invitations may arrive to be a guest in a particular house – often several invitations at a time. Social talent has to be mobilized so as not to offend those who are too late with their offers.

And then comes the night. Formally it is called "Bible evening". I made three errors at my first one. I had not dressed up. All the others had. I tried to initiate a conversation before it all started. The tradition is a joint solemn reflection. And I brought no Bible. But for other reasons too it was an evening I still remember, together with many others. Just to be there, quiet at the beginning. Twelve people. Some of them with strange bodily movements in their daily life, now very quiet. So were also tongues that sometimes ran faster than thoughts, or tongues one felt were not able to communicate insights that actually were there. Through silence we became equal.

Later the text for the service of the following day was read. Read, and discussed. And again it was a united discussion, one between equals. There were no experts on the Bible around. And who are the experts? If one believes that bodies are the carriers of souls, and that souls are there from far back in time, then it is not so obvious that the carrier of any one soul – any one body – is more to be listened to than any other carrier. And the Bible is a treasury of ambiguity. Before the conversation a light meal, then a joint farewell, and the best of all nights was over.

Sundays are different. A large majority assembles for a service. As far as I could find out, there was no particular pressure on anybody to do so; it was more a matter of course. In the service there is music and singing. And that is where they are, all the others one likes to meet. The roles of service-holder and his or her assistants are mostly carried out by co-workers in the village. This is a moment when the hidden authority structure of the village becomes visible. This is accentuated by the ritual of the believers standing up for a moment, confirming their beliefs in a sort of communion, while the others remain seated – a social situation based on exclusion. I preserved my ambivalence towards this by excluding the service from my Sunday program. Afternoons were good for common walks; evenings often had concerts or lectures.

5.3 Celebrations

Saturdays and Sundays give some sort of peak experiences of the week. Other days give peak experiences of the season and the year. There are many such peaks in the villages. Here are the major ones:

New Year's Eve – a gathering at midnight
Carnival – which literally means farewell to carnemeat. A great celebration in the villages.
Lent – when excesses in food are avoided
Easter – always with the performance of one, two or three plays
Whitsun – also with plays
Midsummer – a huge feast to celebrate the long Nordic day and the performance of a play
Advent – which means "arrival" – the period waiting for the arrival of Christ – always with a huge ceremony for children, and with one more candle lighted as each week passes. On the last Sunday in Advent all houses take out their by now very dry decorations of pine or flowers and make a big fire of them at the very same place where they make a fire on Midsummer night. It is dark and cold – and half way towards Midsummer.
Christmas – Celebrations, several plays

All these celebrations are also open to people in the neighbourhood – and also from more distant quarters. Concerts are often announced in newspapers. On "open days" thousands of visitors arrive.

There is also another wheel in the villages – the personal one. The day of christening of any new-born babies is a big day in the villages. Birthdays are also always celebrated. So are confirmation and marriages. Quite recently the wheel has been made complete; a graveyard was created. That was not an easy task. A diary was kept of the process. Thirty-two meetings were held, with municipal authorities, with county and state authorities. With priests and bishops. With site visits. With a great amount of coffee. With promises and initiative from the local expert on how to bring gardens into shape. After all this came the victory: official permission to bury the dead in Vidaråsen, just behind the place where the services are held. So the circle is complete. Birth is often given at Vidaråsen; one midwife lived there for a long period, others come when asked. Old people remain. One house will probably be converted to provide special service to disabled people. It will probably also function as a nursing home for the whole municipality. And now a graveyard. Full circle.

5.4 Two types of time

To understand what is described above, we might get help from the two classical concepts of time: cyclical time and linear time.

Cyclical time is the old time. It is time measured through the coming and going of the tide. Cyclical time is measured through the days, through the months, through the female periods, through the seasons of the year, or through the stages of a human's life. Cyclical time is repetitive; next spring the swallows will be back anew, next autumn fruits will ripen. It is a time related to great occasions, with references back in time and with promises for the future. Cyclical time leads one's attention in both directions; towards the future where time moves, but also backwards, so that what is past will appear anew. Maybe this makes it slightly easier to be where one is, somewhere in between the beginning and the end, with a perspective towards both sides.

Linear time has other characteristics. A symbol of linear time is the digital watch. This is a time with even steps towards infinity. Every second a new number is produced, and at the same moment the old one has disappeared. Time is chopped up into small equal pieces. It is a time coming from infinity, and moving towards infinity. It is sometimes claimed that linear time is close to the male perspective while cyclical time is "female time".

Linear time directing one's attention towards the future might tempt one into a sort of disregard for history. This might lead to a tendency to live in the future. It is not today that counts, but tomorrow. I invest in today – and postpone gratifications – in order to be able to eat the fruits some day in the future. It is the life of the industrious capitalist, efficiently symbolized through the functions of the digital watch. Time is valuable. Batteries have to be bought, and the used ones thrown away. Time is exactly what Benjamin Franklin said. It is money. This is the major tendency. It is the industrialized linear adaptation.

Quite obviously, the villages are deeply embedded in cyclical time. The small wheels of the day, the repetitions in them and of them. The small peaks at the week-end and the big ones of celebration. Villagers are anchored in the past, by having been there so often, but are also preparing for the future, where they have also been. Leaving the large Hall after the Easter play I hear one strong producer of the play whisper her instruction to some bystanders: Next week they have to join in the preparations for the performance to be given at Whitsun.

5.5 Free time

I have for a long time been in the habit of asking people what they do when they are not working. What they do in their "free time". I ask, not in order to get to know the specific details, but the more general concepts they apply. A clear pattern of contrast emerges, captured in the two concepts

vacation and holiday

Most are on vacation, of one sort or another. Often they only define it as a negation of labour or work: I am not working, I have time off, I am free, I am resting, vegetating, taking it easy. A much smaller minority will say: I am on holiday, I am off to celebrate.

Listen again to the message of these words.

Vacation, that means empty time, time without content. Vacancy – empty position. The vagrant is a man permanently on vacation. The rich English gentleman of the last century is another example of the species, only so well trained that he filled the empty time with cultural or recreational actitivities. He illustrates at the same time that it takes much money, a long time, and considerable suffering in public school and universities to cope with situations of vacant time. Vacation is thus a sort of escape; it is a move away from something, from labour.

Holiday is more of a positive goal. "Ferie" is an alternative Scandinavian/German word. Its closeness to "feire"/"feiern" – that is celebration – is obvious. Or rather once it was obvious. Vacations were not vacations, but celebrations – of Christmas – Easter – Midsummer Night, and of important points in individual biographies. The work had to wait pending the celebrations of Christ's nativity, or on a smaller scale pending the celebrations of one's relatives. It was often a strain to leave the work or the "verk". Edvard Munch, the Norwegian painter, has described his feeling of despair when he was supposed to meet his sister for coffee. He was tortured by the thoughts of what sort of work – what sort of masterpieces – he could have created if he had not been obliged to join the family-setting.

When sufficiently self-conscious people in our society are close to their 50th, 60th, or 70th birthday, it happens that they inform the mass-media that they do not wish any mention to be made of the event. This has been made into a system. It is possible to pay to avoid any publicity, a small amount to the national news agency, which then transmits the announcement to all newspapers, radio stations and TV that the person in question does not want to be mentioned. Many people also leave town on big days of celebration. Or they are left to their inner circle of relatives on their last possible celebration – the funeral. Announcement of this potential celebration does often state that flowers are not desired, or even that the burial has already taken place. What a contrast to the state of affairs in Christian IV's time. This Danish-Norwegian king died in 1648, but had to remain in his coffin – unburied – for ten months waiting for the completion of funeral preparations worthy of such a great ruler.

And why do we not celebrate? Because we have nothing to celebrate. And why do we not have anything to celebrate? Because we have nothing to associate around – for example celebration. Social interaction is the fertile ground for celebration, and celebration is the stimulant to interaction. But interaction comes first.

Celebration occurs between such people as have something in common, something to be in common about. For a time one can

continue on the basis of old habits, but then the traditions become
more pale, absence due to illness increases, relatives do not want
any attention . . .

Village life is life in a multitude of interrelated wheels. A beginning, an end, and maybe once more a beginning. Full circle.

5.6 Revolt

Some years ago a revolt took place at Vidaråsen.

The village had tried to modernize. Everywhere else life was organized according to modern times – fast, efficient, concentrated.
There was no longer room for the long midday intermission. No
siesta. The machinery of industrialized society cannot be left idle
for hours in the middle of the day. And when the activity is
labour, not work, it is in everybody's interest to get it all done in
one concentrated effort so that real life can commence. Vacation.
In Vidaråsen it was argued that a shortening of the long midday
break would give more time for creative cultural work in the afternoons and evenings. Therefore, the midday intermission was cut
to half, and everybody went home an hour earlier in the afternoon.

It lasted from summer to Christmas. Then came the storm. At a
village meeting several people – most of them supposed to be severely deficient – rose and demanded to get the old time back.
They had two complaints against the new time. First, work became so hectic. The pleasure in work vanished. Secondly, and this
seemed to be the major point: It became so difficult to meet other
people in the village, particularly those supposed not to be handicapped. It was as if they all disappeared just when work stopped.

Of course they disappeared. The new rhythm was adapted to industrialized living, and the humans adapted to the new possibilities given. Work became labour, time out of labour became vacant – and to be filled according to personal interests. A process
of private entrenchment commenced. Reading, lonely walks, visiting far away. Valuable activities of a type taken for granted in society in general. Life in the village became more similar to life in
the ordinary society. The gains from this were intended, but not
the costs in loneliness among those not suited to industrialized living.

As so often, what happened in the village is only an illustration of what has happened in society at large. Organization of time is a result of power. Concentration of the time used on labour gives a sort of double profit to those of us most able to adapt. With reference to the demands of labour, we can escape many obligations in other arenas. In addition come long periods of vacation when it is possible to hide completely. Saturdays and Sundays and throughout the long vacations a great part of the elites leave for their various hideouts. At home are left the very old, the sick, the maladapted, and youngsters unwilling to be away from those most important of all – other young people. A revolutionary social reform would be to abolish all long vacations and to reintroduce work on Saturdays, but at the same time reduce the numbers of daily hours in paid work. A four to five hour day, 6 days a week, 50 weeks a year, would mean more to the old, to the strange, to the other special categories, than any other reform possible to envisage.

Vidaråsen had its revolt. An agreement was made to go back to the old system with a long midday break. It should be done for a trial period of one year. Several years have now passed and I have heard no suggestion of renewed attempts to modernize. But I still meet villagers who tell me about the miserable period when work became labour.

Saturday off represented another case of modernization. Again it was obvious. Everywhere else Saturdays were a vacation, so why not here too? But in the village this meant trouble. Basically the houses were clean when Saturdays came. This was the job for the workers who came in during the other weekdays. Shopping is the other major measure against empty time in societies like ours. But this is not a good option in villages where private property is given low priority. So Saturday mornings were actually experienced by many as empty time. It came as a relief to many when work till Saturday midday was reintroduced.

6

Culture

6.1 Basic ideas

Five major ideas are often expressed in these villages. First, the importance of an active communism, not in theory, but as a practice in personal life. Secondly, and related to the first, comes communal living. Thirdly, the idea of reincarnation. And fourthly, an acceptance of the importance of what we could call the intellectual project, particularly of life-long studies.

The *communism* is of an old-fashioned type, formulated by Rudolf Steiner in 1905. The core sentences are these:

> The welfare of a group of people who work together is all the better, the less each single person claims for herself or himself the profit of the labour. This means that the more of her or his proceeds which is rendered to other co-workers, the more of her or his own commodities are covered by the labour of others and not by her or his own work.

This is the idea behind the money in the hat principle and the sharing between the villages.

The idea of communal living is based on a long historical tradition. Karl König (1960) traces it back to a little book from the year 1610 on societies of religious brothers (The Order of the Rose Cross), but he might as well have gone back to the oldest Christian communities. In particular he links it to four great thinkers and reformers:

Johann Amos Comenius	(1592–1670)
Count Ludwig Zinzendorf	(1700–1760)
Robert Owen	(1771–1885)
Rudolf Steiner	(1861–1925)

Comenius, famous for his educational ideas, was for a long period the most important teacher for the whole of Europe, and a bishop of the Bohemian Moravian Brotherhood. Zinzendorf continued that work and formed congregations and brotherhoods all over Europe. Together these two thinkers and reformers represented a deep undercurrent of alternative Christianity. This undercurrent was a target for continuous surveillance and attack from the Pope. This was counteracted with social forms emphasizing communal living, sharing of resources, and acceptance of internal differences in confession among those living together. Robert Owen is generally seen as the founder of the socialist tradition in Great Britain. He was himself an industrialist, but had elaborate ideas on how to counteract the evil sides of that system. His own industries became models, for a period highly regarded by everybody. Later the establishment in England and elsewhere turned against him, and he was driven closer to Labour, though always with an ambivalent relationship. In 1821 came his utopian principles on cooperative villages for farming and industry. Several were created, both in Great Britain and in the USA. The similarity to the Camphill villages is striking when Rudeng (1980 vol. 5, p. 68, my translation) describes some of the activities built up:

> . . . a radical political culture with alternative communal houses ("Halls of Science"), journals, books of songs, ceremonies of marriages, e.g. were created. Festivals were arranged. Here large physical and chemical experiments, dancing, and drinking of tea took place. Technology and natural science were of major importance. The movement included shoemakers and other craftsmen who wrote books on socially responsible ways of applying new technical developments and on convenient ways of organizing production and collectivities for living. Ideas on biodynamic farming and ecology were anticipated. Likewise ideas on energy from wind, sun and the tides.

The third basic idea is the one that bodies are only provisional carriers of the much more permanent element – the soul. A strange belief in our time. But it is our time that is strange, not the idea. *The belief in reincarnation* appears in many cultures, and it is an idea with interesting social consequences. Particularly it is an important idea when there are many extraordinary people around. Some may irritate through their behaviour. Some represent quite a break with usual standards of how to behave and how to look. Some faces might at first glance seem rather repulsive, and at least unaesthetic. For people close to them these traits will soon be of small importance. The idea of reincarnation gives an impetus in the same direction. It gives a reminder that the body is only the wrapping. Inside is a dignified soul – soon to continue in another body. If it is a question of accepting or rejecting the idea of reincarnation, those who accept ideas of this sort will probably have an advantage in their relationships with extraordinary people.

The fourth common idea is the belief in *the importance of studies and intellectual involvement*. These villages, where so many cannot read nor write, are basically strongly intellectually oriented. Wherever and whenever one comes, there are study-circles, seminars, courses or lectures going on. Those able to do so travel extensively to other places of learning, which often means other villages, but also to national or international meetings arranged inside or outside the villages. Vidaråsen is continuously the host for seminars on medicine, economy, or for festivals in music or dancing. Living in or visiting the villages I am again and again struck by being more among intellectuals in these villages than at any University I know. There is a burning curiosity in the village. A will to find out. A willingness to sacrifice for that purpose. Cultural programs for everybody several nights a week, often with extra study-groups after most people have gone to bed. Tired, contracted eyes in the morning, then a long day of hard work in the fields or in other places of work, in the bakery, but then half an hour of reading sneaked in through the midday intermission, – and then a long tour with villagers to attend an evening concert in Oslo in the evening.

The fifth basic idea came to the surface as a result of circulating a preliminary manuscript of this book. Describing Sundays in the villages, I had written that a large majority goes to the church. The reaction was explosive: "For Heaven's sake, we have no church!" Then I tried "chapel", a term I had heard used in British villages. But again I missed. The British were all wrong on this point. "So, what do you want me to call the house that is not a church nor a chapel?" "Call it 'Andreas-bygget', the name we originally gave that building."

Of course, I ought to have seen it. Deep in the village culture is a distrust towards formal classificatory systems and an attempt to evade terms such as mentally retarded, staff, doctors, assistants, directors. Equally deep is a wish not to be captured in dogmatic classificatory systems when it comes to religion, culture or politics.

The village has no church. It has a house with a name to it. It has no priest, only a person with a personal name who performs the service. It has no director, but a person who signs the letters. It has no staff, but active persons. It has no pensioners, only people who do some sort of work as long as they have some strength left. And there are, as far as it is possible to press the idea, no mentally retarded or insane living in the village, only persons. Categories inherited from the society in general, and from the various professional groups in particular, are dangerous for the development both of ideas and of human potentialities.

In Karl König all these ideas converge. When he founded the first school for children in need of care, he was a refugee in England. In his own words (König 1935, reprint 1960, p. 9):

> There was, from the beginning on, a task which we had set before us: Curative Education. Some of us were trained in this work and the rest were willing to grow into it. We felt it as a special kind of mission to bring this work about. We had learned from Rudolf Steiner a new understanding for the handicapped child and we had seen this work in several homes and schools on the Continent and in Great Britain. To add another place to those already existing, was our first goal.
>
> At the same time, we dimly felt that the handicapped children, at that time, were in a position similar to ours. They were refugees from a society which did not want to accept them as a part of their community. We were political, these children social, refugees.

6.2 Another heritage

Sometimes while living in the village or thinking of the villages, pictures appear in my mind. Other settings, other times. A girl, black hair, speaking a slightly broken Norwegian, violin, a foreign bird in the Oslo bourgeoisie. Some families I had lived with in the USA. Small encounters in Jerusalem and Tel-Aviv. And then, as a revelation, the book by Mark Zborowski and Elizabeth Herzog (1952): *Life is With People. The Jewish Little-Town of Eastern Europe.*[1]

The book is an anthropological study of a culture which no longer exists, says Margaret Mead in her preface (p. 10). I think

1 I am grateful to Berthold Grünfeld for bringing this book to my attention.

she is wrong. Reading Zborowski and Herzog is a continuous reminder that parts of the culture exist, but in other wrappings. The reading is a continuous reminder of life in the Camphill villages. Not because the villages are Jewish. They are not. Not because the villagers are particularly interested in those theological problems that preoccupied the Jews. Not because they are particularly poor, discriminated against, or oppressed. But because they share the respect for the importance of intellectual development and a life in learning, and because their cultural and social forms exhibit striking similarities.

In the Jewish little towns – the shtetl – or in those parts of the towns where the Jews lived, time was not vacant. Children started school when they were three or four; the day in school lasted from eight o'clock until six, in higher education four or five hours of sleep away from the books were deemed necessary. Synagogues were synagogues *and* universities. All men of rank used all available time for reading or discussions. There were also among them a large segment belonging to the lower class who participated in the rituals, but not personally in the intellectual life. But also for them the ideals were clear: Held in greatest esteem were those who had cultivated their intellect more than any others. Men of knowledge walked solemnly, a symbol of deep reflection, had worn eyes except in deep intellectual discussions where they glittered intensely, and were used as advisers in all practical as well as in moral matters. Their exams were the daily encounters.

The celebrations in the shtetl also bring reminders of the villages. The Sabbath evening is seen as the foretaste God gives of the future world. Preferably a guest will attend, because without a guest no Sabbath is truly complete. As stated by Zborowski and Herzog:

> One who does not fulfil the commandments of Sabbath, sins against the entire Law. But the gratification of Sabbath, the opportunity to escape the "vokh" [everyday life, "hverdagslig" in Norwegian, N.C.], to devote a full day to the family, and to the community, and to the most beloved activity, study of the Law, exalts the devout Jew of the shtetl. It fills his heart with joy and pride, and also with pity for his neighbor, the peasant, who – free from the anxious burden of Sabbath prohibitions – is also deprived of enjoying the blessed contrast between Sabbath and vokh. (Zborowski and Herzog 1952, p. 60).

So back to the villages: their Bible evening has qualities comparable to the Sabbath. The tranquillity combined with the good discussion. The guest attending, the ritualized meal. Next day to the service, most often with a lecture in the evening. And then for those with the highest rank the emphasis on studies of the Bible and of the books of Rudolf Steiner, the founder of anthroposophy.

Steiner was an unbelievably productive author, and he had a group of persons surrounding him who wrote down most of his lectures. It has been estimated that there exist some 50 books amd 4000 articles and lectures by Steiner (Hansman 1989). Not all of them are equally crystal clear. Just as in the Bible, there is room and need for interpretation. He wrote on architecture and created buildings. He wrote on education and created schools. He wrote on medicine, and followers created hospitals. He wrote on farming, and out came biodynamic farms. He wrote on new ways of social organizations, and the villages attempt to some extent to arrange life accordingly. And he wrote on occult matters, scripts eagerly studied by many anthroposophists all over the globe. In summary: Rudolf Steiner and his followers have an exceptionally large production with a range from the most mysterious wisdom over to pedantic concrete descriptions on how to blend cement. It is relevant for most areas of life, often open to different interpretations by the readers. And all the time with an explicit and also implicit message that it is a prime responsibility for the human being to cultivate her or his abilities.

It is stretching the analogy far to compare the shtetl to the villages and the Torah to Steiner's writing. There are also extreme differences. The villages are not male-dominated; on the contrary, females have an exceptionally strong position there compared both to the shtetl and life in the ordinary society. And the villages put no emphasis on belonging to any particular race or folk. On the other hand; Jews and those who know them will understand more of the villages through this analogy, and others might understand more of Jews. And I have one more point in defence of the analogy: the history of the villages.

The founder was Karl König. He was a very successful doctor in Vienna, a Christian by religion, but with Jewish parents and a childhood in the old Jewish part of Vienna. With a group of friends he developed ideas on how to create a new society in Nazi-threatened Austria. Then came Hitler, and most of the group was dispersed, but met again in Great Britain. Here the first school for handicapped children was founded. From this stems the village movement called Camphill. The group from Vienna were the founders. Leading personalities had a Jewish background. They had converted to Christianity, but they were children of the Shtetl. They were brought up in a tradition of communal living, in the village converted into total collective living. They were accustomed to the Sabbath evening, in the village converted into the Bible evening. And they were formed with a deep respect for studies – converted from Torah into anthroposophy. In addition came the other impulse from the old Christian communities, from the society of brothers and from Zinzendorf. König's wife belonged to that tradition, and seems to have been very influential in strengthening both the aestethic impulse and also the ritual forms that can be found in the daily life of the villages.

6.3 The village as a university

Each year a rather extraordinary seminar takes place in Norway. It is arranged for and by people who officially are called mentally retarded and/or have other severe disorders that make them eligible for some sort of state pension. The program is decided by them, so are most of the practical arrangements and nearly all contributions during discussions.

I have several times had the good luck to be invited by the villagers to give a lecture at these seminars. And when I say good luck, I mean good luck. Let me explain why.

When one is lecturing to those who maybe are not able to follow all the words, or who might need more time than usual to follow all sorts of verbal reasoning, it is important immediately to move towards the centre of any problem. The major theme must be the major message. If punishment is the topic, then intentional infliction of pain must come in the centre, and be made concrete as by Foucault (1977) on torture or by Seip (1946), the then elected Rector of the University of Oslo, on how he felt at being publicly caned in a German concentration camp. Likewise, if justice is the topic, the various philosophers cannot be allowed to occupy the centre of attention. In the centre there must be concrete examples of dilemmas of justice, linked together in major sentences.

Like so many university people, I have a problem during ordinary lectures. Time becomes too short. There is so much to say. References, quotations, related ideas, the old giants who have to be given their due credit. After years within the field one knows a lot. Challenged in a situation with ordinary people, or rather extraordinary ones, all this changes. All of a sudden it is not obvious any more that all I know is worth knowing. But small parts are important. These small parts, the essence, are forced to the forefront when the exceptional people are there.

But in this way one is forced back to a most old-fashioned situation. One is forced back to the *University* as it functioned when those working there still had possibilities to meet and to converse on common interests. Few sciences, few teachers. So few that they were forced towards each other and thereby towards the universal.

Extreme growth is the fate of modern universities. This growth makes fertile ground for specialization. With specialization follows increased possibilities of spending all one's time with colleagues within the speciality. At the same time the experience of a need to explain the central points, and why they are central, evaporates. "University" is the wording of the letter head. Cafeteria for elements of knowledge might be more precise. With the extraordinary people from Vidaråsen as the audience, I feel more like a university professor than in any other setting.

In addition to seminars by and for those supposed to be retarded, I have also lectured relatively often to mixed groups. Some extraordinary people, some more usual. One term I gave joint lectures at the University for my "ordinary" students and a group from Vidaråsen. The topic was principles of justice. Some students dropped out very soon. They might have found the lectures uninteresting, or the company undignified. Other students stayed on and expressed gratitude. They claimed they had gained more than usual with regard to the topic. Particularly they appreciated that so much time had been spent on the core of the problems. My own feeling was that I at last had dared to be sufficiently elementary. I am probably not the only lecturer who sometimes panics and thinks that all I intend to say is obvious. Down there in the far corner of the audience is a student I know as brilliant. And over there is one who followed my lectures two terms ago, probably they know it all. Instead of explaining I turn to short declarations. Instead of reasonings the students receive headlines and categories. With people of all sorts in the audience it is easier not to panic. Attempts to explain might be unsuccessful. But attempts are made.

In addition comes the enthusiasm. With an audience of extraordinary people from the villages there is often created friendliness, a sort of open receptivity, enthusiasm. Some might laugh at points unexpected to me. Some will move their bodies in unexpected rhythms, some will emit sounds where silence would otherwise reign. But there is an atmosphere of contaminating joy in the audience. Among some a joy just to be there, as a part of a totality, enjoying the common enthusiasm. Others might enjoy a joke in the lecture and eagerly wait for the next, while others enjoy the reasoning, the struggle to be able to understand and the pleasure in the insights gained. Warm feelings, good vibrations – a good climate for learning.

Sometimes, when lecturing for the village people, I feel the same as when lecturing in Berkeley some time after 1968. The same curiosity. The same joy. Feelings which are not turned inward, but are generously shared in a common and sometimes very stimulating enthusiasm. I remember Professor Paul Lazarsfeld on one of his visits to Oslo telling a circle of slightly disbelieving Norwegian academics about the enthusiasm among American students. One of them had patted his back, exclaiming: "That was a damned good lecture, professor." Rare actions among ordinary Scandinavian students. But usual among the unusual.

6.4 Villagers as students

But is this really true? Do they understand? Are they not only polite excuses, so that the supposed normal ones can enjoy life and lectures and believe it is good for the villagers as well? Are they not only pretending, filling up the lecture hall, or listening to music of no relevance to them?

I cannot know for sure. But what I *can* say, out of bitter experience, is that the villagers are discriminating. I have had severe defeats as a lecturer in the villages. Lectures of no interest, lectures with no response from the audience. Just politeness. These defeats were caused by two opposite reasons. On the one extreme I got trapped in the academic embroideries, particularly in following the tradition of spending a lot of time on telling them about what I was going to say, and making references to all others who had touched the field. The other defeat was on the entertaining side. For fear of boring the audience I dropped certain complications or packed them into jokes which served only as jokes, not as relevant illustrations of points in the lectures. Victories came when I dared to come direct to the point, to be serious, and as far as possible to present the reasoning as small concrete stories or allegories. Helpful are also concrete illustrations.

In addition comes a more deep possibility. How can we know how to reach each other? Through concepts, through sounds, through the atmosphere created, through meetings of vibrations between humans very much alive? The day before I wrote this, I got an invitation from a friend to an exhibition of her paintings. In the invitation she quotes these words from the author Gunnar Ekelöf (1957, my translation):

> I do not believe in influence, but in identification. One recognizes the number of one's own foreign legion, one's own cell of the secret defense movement. There are of course traditions within art which bind themselves to á superfluous evaluation as to how it came into being etc. But there exists only *one* tradition, the inner . . . on which there is not more to say than that there is a language from one soul to another.

Humans who are different are often as living secrets. We do not quite know. So-called autistic children are in many ways the most pronounced mysteries. What goes on in there, why don't they talk, explain? Or as Eva, diagnosed once as deeply retarded. Her shy smile in certain situations. Her strategies to keep her favourite chair in the living room. Her clear signals when her rights are threatened.

Two major alternatives can be envisaged in communication with exceptional people. Either they are *deficient* (they have a defective machinery and therefore cannot be reached more than on the rudimentary level). Or they are *just different*, another sort, with equipment for other types of communication. Scientific proofs will never be established to help with these questions. We have to find other criteria to decide which hypothesis we will accept. A major criterion is to be found in the usual ethics for coping with doubts: If in doubt, select the alternative best for those parties with least power. If in doubt, do not declare the suspect guilty. If in doubt, don't think of others as deficient non communicators.

6.5 Consumer or producer?

Entering most institutions for those classified as mentally handicapped, one will find a TV-set very centrally situated and vibrating continuously if any program is on the air. The handicapped cannot come to the world, but the world comes to her or him. Modern technology has torn down the walls, made the handicapped more aware of what happens. According to the Ministry of Health, it is a human right for mentally handicapped to have access to TV. Let us quote the Ministry:

> If special conditions do not indicate the contrary, then it must be a clear right [for clients within this area] to have his own TV in the room. If the use disturbs neighbours due to high volume, the user must accept certain restrictions on the use, eventually that the set is taken away. On the other hand it is clear that an institution cannot put forward a general prohibition against TV in the client's own room. (2 September 1981)

The decision was part of an answer to a local director of the state system for the mentally retarded. He had (at that time) also the right to inspect a Camphill village in his county, and disliked intensely most of what went on there, particularly that TV is banned from all villages.

And what happened?

Nothing. TV is still banned from all the villages, except in the room of a deaf person.

The major reasons for the ban were given in a letter from the village in question to the local director in November 1981. The essence of the answer was that TV would kill the social life in the village.

> In the villages we try to stimulate personal initiative and interpersonal contact. TV works against these goals . . . Usually it is a problem in institutions that they offer too little of stimulating activities. In such a situation it is quite understandable that TV is retained. But in the village the situation is the opposite. Cultural and social activities go on nearly every evening . . .

The villages are based on action and interaction. Televison is based on reception and consumption. Television represents a model whereby many receive a product produced by few people, a product easily digested. It is a model in harmony with the major ones of the industrialized society. It is quite obvious that television would have detrimental effects on the social systems of the villages. It is easier to consume than to produce.

But the local director has a point, and so also has the Ministry. Most citizens perceive it as a matter of course to watch TV. Many school children spend more time in front of the screen than at school. Elderly people often have the TV images as their only company. Who is to say that those living in villages are not to watch? It has also to be admitted that the ban on TV is based on a slight disbelief in the strength of the village culture. Is there not sufficient strength in this culture, to make TV lose in the competition for attention? Are villagers going to theatres just for lack of alternatives?

The matter has been discussed again and again in the village assembly as well as in the individual houses. Generally there seems to be a negative attitude to television. But there are opposing voices. Nearly all are accustomed to television when they visit private homes outside the villages. Several want to watch their favourite programs. Villagers supposed not to be mentally retarded or disturbed are, however, all against television. To them television is a tranquillizer. Such drugs are not welcome in the villages. Here the matter rests and will probably remain in the foreseeable future.

6.6 To be another being

Last year 13 different plays were performed at Vidaråsen. Some were repeated on several evenings. All through the year life is filled with preparations for plays leading up to the peak experiences, the performance in the big hall.

All participate. There are roles for all in the imaginary world of the theatre. Kings and devil, witches, mute soldiers, concentration camp prisoners at the edge of starvation, members of processions. I have only participated once, and hated every second of it.

I was a shepherd in the Christmas play. I had refused to be a SS-officer the month before. Now the pressure was irresistible. But I have a handicap. I am almost unable to learn any text by heart. This one was only four lines, in verse. Illogical lines, I will insist. I carried them along for days on a small piece of paper in my pocket. Tried to remember the sequence of the words. We were four messengers, so I hoped nobody would notice if I only moved my lips. Z – the runner – was one of the four. He was able to remember the text, but panicked and ran away just before we were to start. Karl had a speech impediment and kept mute. The third messenger, Karen, was from Denmark. She rescued us. The text came out in one clear Danish voice, and my inadequacy became obvious to all. An extra burden was that so many interpreted my failure as a moral one, as if I had not made any attempts to learn the text, I *had*.

Reflecting on this experience, several years later, I feel it as a triple failure. I am not able to learn by heart. That is the first one. But worse, I did not dare to admit it. I felt terribly embarrassed by being forced to expose my handicap; it was not a natural part of myself. And thirdly, I obviously have trouble in leaving my usual status. This might be the reason for my inability to learn four lines by heart. But it might also indicate a rigid self-satisfaction with present status and a hesitancy in following other tracks. Maybe participation in plays is most important for developments among those of us with most to lose. Villagers dared to take part in it all. Z fled, I was embarrassed. We seem both to be in particular need of village life.

7

Personification of Life

7.1 Rhythm and roads

Between the houses in Vidaråsen runs a complicated network of tracks and roads. Here one can follow the pulse of the village. Cars are discouraged; there is a huge parking-lot outside the village. There are small lamp-posts along most roads and tracks. They are just one metre high so as not to compete with the stars above; they give only a bleak shimmer of light on the surface of the road. Roads and tracks invite walking. So does the social organization: Most people leave the houses in the morning for work in workshops or other houses, then home for midday, out again, home for the evening, and out again for cultural activities. This physical communication system becomes a system for continuous interpersonal communication; it becomes an unavoidable arena for repeated interaction. The network of tracks and roads is an important condition for village life.

From the windows one can observe one of the main results of the network; the *intermixture* of all sorts of people. Those supposed to be dumb in conversation with those who have no pension for disabilities. The major teacher in eurhythmics – a sort of educational dancing – a lady of 87 – helped on the ice by a gallant arm from one of the bakers. Two other persons in slow movement. The one slow because of a leg deficiency, the other because she is from a country unaccustomed to icy roads.

7.2 Limits to dichotomies

This network, combined with the variation in tasks for all in the villages, means that people meet all the time. Continuously they cross each other's paths. Being polite people, they exchange words. Being rational people, they talk about what they think. Those with no qualifications for being special will often feel particular responsibilities. Terje has no place to go this summer, could we include him in the tour to Yugoslavia? Selma Lagerlöf's house will be nearly empty next week-end; might those remaining have their dinner at Ole Bull's house? John is sad because Jane has teased him, could you tell Jane? Of course, matters are discussed. Discussed and often solved. Discussed as they would have been in institutions, but with one fundamental difference: In the villages discussions are to a large extent shaped as natural encounters. In the institutions they become formal meetings. Staff meetings formalize a distinction between "us" and "them". Staff meetings are formally called to solve problems. John and Jane thus become objects for expert-discussions, they become clients. Encounters on the track do not symbolize formal authority; they are not arranged, they give no status, and limits are thereby set to the process of reification – making persons into things – so unpleasant in most organizations run by professional experts.

Often one hears from those working in institutions that so much time is spent at meetings. Of course it is. And rightfully participants complain that they don't have time to see the clients. They do not have time, because they are in meetings where they create clients. The solution is not necessarily more staff. The answers are to be found in ideas, and an organizational practice that breaks down the dichotomy, the "us and them", the subject and the object, the professional and the thing.

7.3 A painting by Brueghel

To come to the villages is like coming to the market in mediaeval times. Paintings by Brueghel are as if taken from Vidaråsen.

Outside the villages most of us live side by side with people of considerable similarities. Same class, same education, same type of work, neighbourhood and taste in wine. Here it is also as if humans homogenize even their appearance. Face, hair, clothes, presentation of self in everyday life, – all to appear as one. It becomes a disappearance through similarity.

Village people go the other way, their own way. As years pass, it is as if they shrug off more and more of the usual, the veneer of ordinary life. The villages have their special days of carnivals, but in a way they have them every day.

Walking the streets of major cities I am often struck by a vague similarity in those I see there to those I know from the villages. This fellow has something of Ola, this lady a trait of Karin. But when in the villages I never find similarities to those I know in town. Those in the villages are characters, so strong that nothing becomes similar when you see them. One can find reminders of their traits in pale counterparts living outside, but not reminders of the pale counterparts when back in village.

People do not become characters without reason. I have already pointed to one: *the limits to dichotomies* in the villages. Staff and clients, these are strong roles, often symbolized by differences in clothing, but also in bodily appearance. Professional training, or semi-professional, is also a training in appearance. Clients of all sorts also learn how to behave as clients; the de-learning of this is often one of the difficulties of a return to ordinary life. The village communities have ideas that counteract the dichotomy, and they live in a physical setting which minimizes the unavoidable parts of it.

Another major condition for the appearance of the Brueghel-motif is the extreme *variation in social history* among those living in the villages. Some arrive from closed institutions, some even from extremely closed ones where they have been perceived as dangerous. Some come straight from mother, very much spoiled, unfit for most tasks until forced by necessities in the village (but then often regressing on visits home). Some have a university degree, but cannot or do not want to function out there; some single parents come with their children to be with many. Most are from Norway, but many are from other countries.

A third major condition for creating characters is *the extreme variation in tasks* carried out by the same persons within the villages. *Peter*: A flute-player in the early morning, responsible for washing the dishes after breakfast, for sales from the pottery throughout the first half of the working-day, a student in a seminar on aesthetics during the afternoon, an absconder in the evening when he was supposed to take part in the village meeting. *Olga*: With some help from friends she got her clothes on and her food in; someone walked her to the doll-workshop and back; in the afternoon with her favourite picture book, but in a bad temper, someone had moved the chair. Evening; the house-mother walked her to the cafeteria, one big smile over the cake. *Leif:* chiming the bells, picking onions, the evening spent with rehear-

sals for the Christmas play. *Anne:* she got her kids ready for the
school-bus this morning too, then replies to letters from applicants
for admission to the village, admits one for a trial visit, receives a
telephone call from a mother, complaining that her "little" daughter (of 32) came home last week-end with terribly dirty trousers.
Sorry, says Anne, but the daughter has to manage this by herself
now, give her time and trust. In the afternoon Anne gets to know
that she has not invested sufficient time in preparing for her part
in the play. In the late evening she attends a meeting on reincarnation. On Sunday she meets most people from the village in the
Andreas building. The message of the service conveyed by people
from the village has to do with equality before God and about
souls that are all dignified.

The consequences of all this, of the lack of dichotomies, of the variation in personal bakground, and of the variations in tasks, is a
personification of life. People meet all the time, but then continuously in new roles. As house-members, as carpenters, as singers,
as guests for dinners, as shepherds in the Christmas play or as tor-
turers in the next play. There are exceptions to the totality of
tasks, but then always with references to earlier stages of life
where the person took part in all sorts of activities. This is all in
striking contrast to city-life where we tend to become our major
roles. The nurse in a local neighbourhood is first and foremost a
nurse, if known at all. The policeman is a policeman. After a
while and with some good luck the nurse is also a bit more than a
nurse, and the policeman more than a policeman. But the roles
remain as major attributes even if the cap and helmet are put
aside. The village people are at the other extreme. They are so va-
ried in history and carry out so many and different tasks visible to
all that it becomes less natural to let one role become the carrier.
Instead, they stand up and out as persons. They reveal themselves
and become types, characters, rather than roles. Roles are open,
they can be performed by several and make these actors predictable. Characters are also predictable, but are not for loan. They
can only be performed by one particular individual. The person.

8

Power

8.1 Who decides?

The villages have no Directors, no King, no Parliament. Who decides?

Formally, it is simple enough. The villages hang together in one foundation with a formal constitution. At the top is the Board of Directors with members from the villages and outside, from Norway and abroad, from ordinary people and less ordinary. They meet twice a year. That is when they decide.

But of course, that is only theory. A Board that used its power would soon be without villages. Decisions are the gasoline of social systems. Village life is based on humans who take an unusual amount of personal responsibility for their own acts, particularly vis-à-vis those close to them. Orders from above remove responsibility. The Boards are, therefore, extremely reluctant in deciding anything that has not been decided beforehand.[1] Before each meeting of the Board representatives from the villages have their own one-day meeting, discussing all matters, forming an opinion on most. These ideas will be evaluated by the Board and mostly accepted. Sometimes doubt is raised, which nearly always results in a postponement until the next Board meeting. Doubts are mostly raised because ideas are not clear enough. This becomes particularly visible at Board meetings with foreign members, at present from Finland, France and Ireland. Their presence creates a situation where we all have to speak English, which is the only language we all have in common. It is a burden, but also a great advantage. Board members say less and with reduced eloquence.

---

1 I can remember two occasions – in a 15-year period serving on the Board – when the Board used its formal power. In both cases I think the decisions, which I then agreed to, were wrong both for the villages and for the persons directly influenced by them.

Problems cannot so easily be glossed over. Proposals sound considerably less convincing; the core of the problem appears. New ideas directly from the Boards might also be brought forward, but only as ideas to be discussed in the villages. Decisions lie with those living with the consequences of them.

Local boards for each village operate in much the same fashion as the general Board. They meet four times a year, survey the local financial situation, and help to clarify matters about which the village inhabitants are in doubt. They operate as a link to the local community. But like the Board they will not decide what is not already decided.

So decisions grow out of the villages. But from where?

Authorities outside the villages wanted to have a formal structure with a director at the top within each village. They have got it – on paper. I think, however, that very few in any village know who is in charge at any time. Directors are for external use. At the moment of writing, I am able to remember who is the director of one of the five villages.

Some would say: power is in the village assembly.

The village assembly is for all. It is a large meeting held every week for all living in the village. Guests often attend. They get a special greeting. So also do newcomers, villagers or co-workers. The assembly has a chairman who directs the discussion. Matters of concern can be taken up during the village meeting, or proposed to the chairman during the preceding week.

The meeting commences with reading of the minutes of the last meeting. The audience pays exceptionally close attention during this reading. The repetition of last week's meeting brings it all back. Protests and comments are frequent from all attending.

Complaints and proposals are many. The roads are icy; they need sand. Strong protest from those who use "sparkstøtting" (a sort of sledge to be pushed on the ice). Shops are not clean enough, people are too late for meals or for work; why have not the dancing classes reopened after vacation, who has taken my bike, what can we do to produce more candles this autumn? Very often people who by many would be classified as deeply disturbed or insufficient, raise questions, good questions. Sometimes those asking for the floor might have speech trouble. The chairman seems to be able to understand and translate the most blurred of speeches. Except from A and B who have their own secret language, languages beautiful to listen to. They receive great applause. One of them, a girl, is completely worn out after her delivery. Sweaty, breathing fast as after a marathon, and smiling happily. She gets the emotional message across.

Often there are confrontations between participants. Harsh words. Sometimes someone cries or leaves the hall. At the last meeting I attended, one villager had an epileptic fit. He was discreetly helped out and home, but without any intermission of the meeting. Epileptic fits are a part of life. Important if given importance. Once a demonstration was staged outside where the assembly was to be held. There had been quarrels on the topic of radios. The demonstrators – led by a person with a Down's syndrome – were in favour of private radios in private rooms. They got their way. The revolt against the unsuitable new rhythm of the day also took place here.

So matters *are* decided on in the village assembly – concrete topics of interest to those attending. Since those living in the villages are so interested in each other, it matters what is said there. There is a great turn-out at the meetings. But some of the most important decisions are not easily handled between so many people: new villages to be established, new villagers to be let in, new houses to be built, new types of relationships to the authorities.

To understand where these matters are decided, we have to turn to the more general base for power in these villages:

There *are* no roles that carry formal power in the villages. But certain categories provide possibilities for gaining more influence than other categories.

Seniority is of importance. Also on this point the villages are in contrast to the ordinary society. The repetitive rhythm of village life makes experience an asset. Those with a long life have a store of the *relevant* knowledge. Limits on dangerous tools mean also a limit to the attraction of the young entrepreneur. Collective living likewise sets limits to fast exposures of material successes. The emphasis of learning is not put on learning "the latest thing", but penetrating eternal problems. And there is no time for retirement in the villages. Participation ends when life ends. Old age becomes a condition, not a handicap. Because of all this, by and large those who have been there for the longest time gain the greatest influence. Formal leaders are also to some extent chosen among these. But seniority is not a guarantee of influence. Three of the founders of the villages in Norway are still living in the villages. All are held in exceptionally high esteem, but only one has strong power extending throughout the whole system.

Kinship might also have been a base for power. Two generations of adults are sometimes living within the systems of villages. A family with four generations present was for some years living in one of the villages. But it is difficult to see these relations as any base for power. Very old persons represent need of care rather than authority. And there do not seem to have developed any particular alliances of power between those generations which are actively working in the villages. Dynastic systems have not evolved.

But *sex* is of importance. By and large, the Norwegian villages are female-dominated systems. Homes are of visible importance. Needs of the households are in the forefront of many discussions. Males participate, but do not dominate. The traditional male territory, the arena of work and technical knowledge, is not gaining any monopoly. On the contrary, considerations of "workers' welfare" are given high priority. Cultural life is filled with themes of equal relevance for males and females. The total result of all this is that these villages do not provide the usual breeding ground for male dominance. In this situation strong females come to the forefront when decisions are made.

My suggestion would be that influence in the village is based on the fulfilment of two demands. First, as a general requirement, to get influence it is necessary to cope with the demand for general participation in all of the three general areas of life; housekeeping, work, cultural activities. To cope with it all, one needs experience. Young people are here handicapped. So also are males.

The second demand is much more difficult to describe in a modern society. It cannot be described as a role. It is a profile. And it has to do with knowledge. But it is not like the profile of a philosopher, or a scientist for that matter, found within usual academic settings. It is not a profile of a person who can concentrate most available time and energy on academic matters. On the contrary, power within the villages is to be found in those persons who *combine the daily concrete demands in housekeeping and work with exceptional energy in a lifelong search for knowledge from that type of literature and art seen as important within the village.* One person in one of the villages had interests and a profile as a scholar, but tended to be a drop-out when the onions were to be harvested. He was initially highly regarded, but then shrank and left the village for a role where he could specialize as a man of knowledge. Other persons in the villages are exceptionally able to cope with practical tasks, in the households or within the workshops. They have great autonomy within these areas. They might install telephones, erect beautiful barns or factories against considerable opposition. They are obviously powerful. But if they are not particularly interested in cultural life, they will have limited possibilities of gaining general leadership.

The most influential person in the villages of Norway these days is a person who combines an earlier and successful performance in all the three major arenas. In particular, her life has been one long search for intellectual answers. She is a life-long student with deep knowledge of the literature regarded as the most important in the villages, particularly the writings of Rudolf Steiner. She is also a charismatic person. Not in the misunderstood meaning of one who can seduce listeners, carrying them away by her oratorical abilities. She can do so, but is often rather dry, with a vocabulary hardly accessible to most people. Her charisma is more in the literary meaning of revealing the message, telling what sort of decisions would be most acceptable according to the general ideas from the old masters. She asks what Goethe or König or Steiner or one of their commentators including herself would have thought, and sticks to that. What the Ministry of Social Affairs thinks, may be food for thought, but not necessarily the last word. Her anchorage in the world of general ideas makes her in many ways uncompromising vis-à-vis authorities outside the villages. Kind, but without sentimentality. Without compromises, but always willing to try really radical alternatives. A believer in God who would love to see a village built up around Buddhistic philosophy. A sceptic, full of beliefs. Such a character is the person who holds most power within the village-movement of the country.

This type of power is one with built-in limits. Again, this is so because of the demand in the villages that all participants have to function in all major tasks. This demand hinders leaders developing who have not been exposed to all sorts of challenges. Some belief systems foster rather peculiar leaders. Fanatics who take their believers from the USA to the Caribbean and there encourage them all to commit collective suicide. Or leaders who abuse their followers, economically or sexually. Or leaders who turn the whole thing into factions of political extremism. But leaders of that type need distance to develop, distance from their followers and distance from the trivialities of everyday life. Confronted with the demand to prove excellency also in the task of changing napkins, to treat the mad with respect, to pick vegetables, to perform as Maria or as a thief in the play, they just cannot make it. The leaders who do emerge in the villages come so close that the whole set of norms of the daily life is activated. If they were to forget norms of care and tender concern, they would not be in a position of leadership. The chances are also great that they will not forget, being that close.

All participants have to function with all tasks. But with this restriction others follow. Particularly, this creates limits to the size of the total system of villages that can hang together. Changing of napkins takes time. Running large systems also takes time. To be tied to the daily tasks means limits to time used in governing others. With growth the system will fragment, which is all for the good. If the network of villages grew large under one coherent system of leadership, things would have to be organized in other ways. Power would be formalized, bureaucracies created, clear lines of command and hierarchical structures established. The rewards built into the present village life would not be there. Work would be labour. Decisions would be made far away. Demands for compensatory rewards would be raised and differentiated salaries reintroduced. Villages would be converted into institutions, and it would all be lost.

8.2 Rewards

All formal organizations we know from the sphere of work have numerous rewards built in. A ladder of promotions, with differences in salaries, in titles, in office space, in equipment provided to do the job. Often people are seated according to rank around tables for lunch or for meetings. The most important member will often arrive last, when they are all ready, so that none of his important time is lost. When the meeting is over, he – it is nearly always a he – leaves before any other. The right to use power is often seen as a part of the reward system. Sometimes it is seen as such an important part that other rewards can be minimized.

The villages have next to nothing of the usual rewards built in. Promotions do not exist, there are no positions to be promoted to. Responsibilities for tasks do exist, but no task is seen as more important than others. And none are allowed to develop as more important. If anybody tends to put too great emphasis on any particular task within the village, that person is often encouraged to leave the area and move into other tasks. The accounting system was to some extent centralized and brought to perfection by one person with a talent for computers. He was gently, and sometimes not so gently, encouraged to go into farm-work instead. The bakery increased its production steadily. This is going too well was the verdict. So large a production of bread indicates that other values are given too little attention. To counteract production, key personnel were given important challenges in the area of cultural life.

The closest one could come to a position of formal rank was probably to be a member of a team of experienced villagers who moved around in other villages to give advice. During the last weeks of writing this book I learned that the team has been dissolved. It was felt that it lessened the importance of the Board of Directors (*Representantskap*). To be a member of that Board is also an indication of trust. But the Board tries to minimize this by inviting everybody who is interested to attend most of the Board meetings. What is free for all, cannot be used as rewards for a few.

An analogy to village life is family life, but then in a special form, a form that combines old-fashioned families and modern ones. Village life resembles *old-fashioned families* in containing many members with common ties. All households are large, and the village as a whole can be seen as an even greater unit of extended kinship. Small celebrations take place in the individual houses, but the large ones are for all living in the village. When a child is born, it is of general concern. The Christening is a public event, with a celebration open to everybody. So is marriage, and so is death. Family life in the village is an open life, with all attending.

The similarity to the *modern family* is in the authority structure. Paterfamilias (mostly in the form of the materfamilias) does exist within some households, but with few visible signs of privileges connected with the position. In some cases can be observed mother or father figures who do not take their equal share of the menial tasks, but usually they take more than their share of these tasks. It is also difficult to establish an authoritarian role in the house. New and mostly young co-workers will appear in the houses. They will come with standards from the surrounding society. They just do not accept the old style, but complain or leave. The villages have had such cases. Many also have children of their own. It is striking, and a matter of surprise, how the ordinary child and youth culture of Norway has put its stamp on these children. The villages have no television, very little of the values of the consumer-society, and great emphasis on spiritual life. But the kids are of the usual sort; often noisy, rebellious, and representing a common culture where any display of old-fashioned authority is flatly rejected. To bring up a child is a soft matter, to help a youngster into adulthood is like getting a salmon up from the river on so vulnerable a fishing rod that it can break at any moment. Authority is of limited use. In addition there is the fact that house parents are continuously short of time. They have their work and their cultural life. The problem in most households is lack of time and will to take responsibility for decisions and necessary work rather than any overdose of authoritarianism.

Rewards in the villages are, therefore, more like rewards in ordinary families of a relatively democratic type, which means there are none, except respect and love. And no hope of anything more. No ceremony for the mother of the year, no particular attention for the father, the aunt, the obedient son. Just ordinary life, led according to ordinary standards. In contrast to formal organizations there is no specification of goals, nor are there rules for how these goals ought to be reached. But lack of specifications for goal attainments means that performance cannot be measured. No winners can be found. "She was a good mother". But why? If children were to sum up during the funeral, they might have trouble in finding an exact explanation of why and how. It was probably something of the atmosphere, the daily flow of daily events, myriads of encounters, hopefully a majority of them good. Within organizations ladders are to be climbed, goals to be reached. Family life is its own purpose. The process is the goal.

In the villages all life resembles family life. This creates one particular problem: What to do with those who get tired of the multi task existence and think they deserve some special attention and rewards? What to do with status-seekers where status is no commodity?

Within other types of social organizations two solutions are used: Such people get honorary positions of some sort, or they are forced to leave the organization. But neither of these solutions is easy to apply within the villages, particularly not the expulsive one. Villages are not easy to leave. It is a unique world with so many attractions that ordinary society will seem meagre fare both for those contemplating leaving, and for those who might wish them to do so. And after years in the villages nobody has money to start a new life. All needs have been cared for, but all surplus money has been plowed back into the village. It is also felt as a breach of one of the most basic rules to push people out if they have been in for long. Villages are for the whole life cycle. This is what the graveyard in the village tells us.

Honorary positions are equally impossible to distribute. No formal rulers exist. This takes the meaning away from honorary appointments. And there is no increase in privileges with increasing age or with particularly good deeds performed. The burden of physical age is so small compared to other burdens visible in abundance within any village. Age is, therefore, an attribute of limited interest. Nobody pays attention to the legal pensionable age. Without usual salaries, and with an abundance of tasks in need of attention, people work with these tasks until they literally cannot function any more. This is all for the good compared to the consequences of age outside the villages, but it is bad if one wishes to use age as a criterion for obtaining privileges.

Those not satisfied with just being decent are thus in trouble, and the village with them. This is the cost of such a system. Honorary positions are not available and cannot be without a breach with the basic demands of general participation and equality in the importance of all tasks.

Villages do not offer possibilities of vertical mobility, but the horizontal one remains open. Both villagers and co-workers move around to a considerable extent. They move inside the village or between villages both in Norway and internationally. Only a minority will have remained in the same house for more than three or four years. Most often individuals or couples move, but sometimes great parts of households. Shifting of place of work also happens. These possibilities for moving seem to function as a sort of safety valve. A household might get sour. A person might be felt as intolerable, or feel that the others are. But a house, or a whole village, might also be in need of a new member. The same is the case with places of work. The moves thus have the advantages of unclarity. They might be the result of a push, but also of a pull; they might be the result of strongly felt needs in the mover to leave or they might be the result of needs in the old household to get rid of the mover, or in the new household to get just her or him. An irritant in one setting might prove a resource in another. An extremely noisy extrovert might be a problem among equals, but a blessing in a very docile household. And here comes the advantage in the fact that all households as well as all villages are organized according to the same basic pattern. A move means new people and new social constellations, but not new forms and rhythms. Many villagers go abroad. They visit foreign villages for days or years. Often they do not speak the language, and are classified by authorities as retarded. But the rhythm and system of the village they come to is not unfamiliar. A few days after arrival they function in the new system.

One other route, of escape or reward, is open to those in the village: It goes into inner depths, meditatively or intellectually. Villages are places for reflection. The small moments of silence before meals and before meetings help participants again and again to correct the course. Village life is a life in turmoil, with an abundance of tasks, with a fight to get it all done in time. Nonetheless, it has at the very same time qualities of tranquillity which give room for moves towards inner resources.

8.3 Social control

In the *Jerusalem Post* last summer came the news of an editor in deep trouble (26 August 1988). His newspaper was one for highly orthodox Jews. One of his articles was unacceptable to them. He was brought before a tribunal. This was the sentence:

> God-fearing residents are warned by the order to stay at least four cubits – 2.4 metres – from Rabbi Haim Katzenellenbogen, head of the Tora V'Yira yeshiva and a leader of the militantly anti Zionist Neturai

Karta. He is not to be counted as a 10th man in a minyan [prayer quo-rum]. He is not to be helped to earn a living beyond that needed for sustenance. It is forbidden to wish him "shalom".

Brutal when formalized. But of course, this is what we all some-times do in daily life. We move close as acceptance and distant as disapproval. Control means counter-roll. In close-knit systems there exist myriads of ways to symbolize disapproval. These ways are in use also within the villages. And they are powerful within villages, more so than in ordinary society. There are few hiding places within villages. Distance is felt because most people of im-portance to oneself are there all the time. Encounters which turn to non-encounters cannot be evaded. The conditions which make it possible to escape the experience of negative informal sanctions are not so easily available in villages.

In addition, four other mechanisms operate within the villages; the village meeting, the celebration of St. Nicholas, changing of house or village, – and finally, expulsion from the village society.

Village meetings are often used to express criticism. Villagers engaged in receiving material for the composts from the house-holds might get fed up with finding bottles and tins and plastic in the garbage. They perform a sketch during the village meeting un-derlining dangerous consequences. Criticism directed towards specific individuals also takes place. "Someone tells lies about me behind my back," says Peter. Eva answers angrily that it was not she who had said it, but Peter ought to come to work on time. A quarrel evolves, and the village meeting listens with interest. An-other complaint is driving of motorcycles on the track. No name is mentioned. It is not necessary, there is only one such cycle in the village.

The day of St. Nicholas is used to its utmost. His day of celebra-tion is on December 6. According to the village this is the real day for distributing gifts to those who particularly deserve them. I got a pair of angel's wings the autumn I lived in the village. In a short speech St. Nicholas told me that I was O.K., but ought to turn my attention slightly more towards heaven. Ellen got a beautiful dress. She has a tendency to turn all her attention to other people's needs, and forget her own appearance. Other people got gifts that were just kind. The whole village attends. Much is told through gifts that evening.

Ostracism is the final move. In the history of the Norwegian villages it is an extremely rare event. The usual procedure is that villagers first come to the villages on a test-visit. But when that period is over and they stay on, the basic idea is that they can stay forever. In a few cases State authorities have forced someone on to the village. There have been people from closed wards and with exceptionally many and noisy problems of behaviour. Villages have not been able to cope. There is also the case of Z, who came straight from prison. After years of turbulence his behaviour vis-à-vis small children became so extreme that he was returned to prison (see page 20). In one case a couple of co workers were formally asked to leave, but one of them continued to work in the village on a salary adapted to wages in the ordinary society. Several young co-workers have been advised to leave, or left on their own initiative, fed up with the village or with particular individuals there. Conflicts are particularly prone to appear over the topic of specialization. It is difficult to accept that anything might be of greater importance than the very task I am the expert on.

Visitors to the villages are often struck by their friendly atmosphere, sprinkled with tranquillity. In a way the impression is right. This does not mean that village life is only peace. Living so close the parties become of extraordinary importance to each other. Emotions run high, both love and hate. It is surprising that it does not end in explosions more often. Part of the explanation is probably the rhythm of village life. Conflicts evolve, anger builds up, in ordinary life explosions would follow. In villages more takes place. Parties meet on all sorts of tasks. If the conflict is within a house, those involved will also meet on the Bible evening. It is a sort of cleansing process, says one villager. An occurrence of great importance. A gathering around topics so large that conflicts shrink in importance. Conflicts do not need to be the topic at all, but they are laid behind when the evening is over. The next day the conflicting parties will probably meet in a communal sermon. Sunday evenings have nearly always music or lectures. Silent moments, art and intellectual challenges create situations where one feels slightly awkward in keeping an interpersonal conflict burning.

This chapter has been a search for power. But in vain. There are no King or Queen, no President, no director worth mentioning, no boards who want to decide, no elections. There are built-in restrictions on specialization; only those who combine qualifications from home life, work life and cultural life have any influence. One has more of it than others, but it is possible to oppose her, and get away with it.

What sort of system is this?

Decisions are made. Farms are bought, houses are built, people are admitted, some are kicked out. Power is exerted, but where is that power?

Again we have to go back to the distinction between society and state, between living communes and ordered categories, between shades and clarity. These villages can be seen as small nests of opposition against the hegemony of state-categorization. They evade usual categories of people as well as of belief system.

But by these insights we have actually advanced. We can say: Power in the village and between the villages is of a type found within relatively open systems with an informal structure. There exist contracts on property – it is all owned by the village trust.

And there is a contract between the State or municipalities regarding funds for those living there paid for by authorities. But regarding those supposed not to be in particular need of care, there are no documents. They just come, stay, or eventually leave again. Up to now, they have had no rights on paper, no contracts, no guaranteed money to take out if they leave. Their personal power rests in their value to the village, and standards of decency and justice shared between those living there.

No guarantees, no clarity, a life beyond contract. It sounds impossible, until we remember that this is the life most people have lived. Always.

9

Rare Species

Walking slowly through a forest, one is faced with mysteries. It might be winter with new-fallen snow. The white powder muffles all sounds. But not totally. A quiet forest is never completely silent. Some winter birds call out, the burden of snow makes the trees sigh. And all over are tracks from the inhabitants. Here the hare has jumped, dangerously close come the prints of a fox; the heavy tail has gently touched the top layer of the snow. And here, these heavy dumps, is it possible that an elk has slept here, so close to town?

To live is to interpret, to give meaning to signs. What sort of phenomenon is this, the plant, the animal, the human, the many humans together? To understand we compare. Footprints with other footprints, social systems with other social systems.

9.1 The villa

While the villages were still very young, a meeting was held within the Ministry of Health. The doctor in charge, a kind man, always acting in defence of the villages, wanted to discuss treatment plans. He raised questions of rehabilitation of the villagers, how to get them back into society at large. And he highly approved of Vidaråsen buying a villa in a nearby town. Here a few villagers with a relatively limited amount of troubles would live together with some of the most experienced house-parents. It was seen as a first step back to society.

The villa proved an immediate success. All who moved there got employment in town. They earned money. They were able to cope with the challenge of modern industry. Their days of work became legendary back in the village.

Their evenings and nights were not so eagerly commented

upon. From work they went home to the villa. Here they were warmly received by the house parents, the elite co-workers. Elite – but the same ones every day. And the same five or six other villagers. The same limited group of people, and the same limited program such a limited group could initiate.

And now they were in town, half way to leaving village life, half way to becoming ordinary people in ordinary city-life, eager for ordinary life with ordinary people. Some neighbours invited them for coffee. But they were old folks, and the villagers felt young. The villagers hunted for equals, ordinary friends, just ordinary.

They hunted where other ordinary people also were hunting. The railway cafe, some snack-bars, open day and night, the harbour. Public places, places of transition for most people, places of hope for those with limits in the network. Cafes cannot be frequented without some sort of consumption. Beer was easily available. Several of the former villagers sailed into troubled waters. Some are still there.

Why did it go wrong?

Seen through the perspective of distance in time, two major reasons can be found. First, the villa was not a village. Secondly, there is no natural room for exceptional people in modern towns.

9.2 Are villages institutions?

The kind doctor was fond of Vidaråsen, as an excellent institution, open for experiments, with lots of human contact. But still, for him, it was an institution. It was not real life. It would therefore as a matter of course be an improvement if humans moved out of the village and into real life.

Those close to the villages have another view. They look at the villages as the real life, maybe extraordinarily real. They agree that life in institutions might often have less satisfying aspects, but claim that the villages are very far from being one. Are they right?

Four attributes are typical of most institutions.

First, most time is spent within a limited geographical area. Work, leisure, sleep – all take place within the same building and with the same people around all the time. This is typical of institutions. And it fits the villages. Here there is communal living, day and night. It is a life in deep contrast to the life led by the ordinary family members in ordinary life where most members leave both home and neighbourhood for work and leisure, and then often associate with several sets of people who do not know the other sets. So, on this account, villages are similar to institutions.

The second characteristic of institutions is the strong differentiation between staff and non-staff. Important staff members claim to be experts. They often have special education. There is the army in white, the doctors and nurses. Or the army with keys, locking up people. Or those with the power of age; the old ones in boarding schools or the young ones in old folks' home. There are those with access to private offices, to staff meetings, to special canteens, or to separate tables in the common canteen. Most often all these staff members have authority over all non-staff.

It is all basic for institutions, but not for the villages. As we saw, various features of village life minimize the difference between us and them: the system of roads and tracks as a functional alternative to staff meetings, the sharing of all tasks, the belief in the dignified soul. And above all: Guards and nurses go home; they leave the limited geographical area. As a matter of course, they have also a life outside the institution; house, family, leisure. Their time in the institution is labour for money. In the village they all remain, some for ever. Living close, acting together, working together, relaxing close to each other. It is a totality, but then a total community, not a total institution. In a paradoxical way the villages are more total than most total institutions described by Goffman (1961). If anything, they are more similar to ships than to hospitals.

A third attribute of institutions is that life there goes on according to a master plan. It is a life with a common, specified purpose. Prisons and hospitals are prime examples, but so also are special homes for children, for students living at the school, for old folks, or for various categories of handicapped persons. Punishment, treatment, education or care become here central purposes.

That villages have not the purpose of punishment goes without saying. Nor are they places for incarceration or isolation in any form. None are prevented from leaving if they so wish. People come there, first for some weeks. If they like it, and the village accepts them, they can stay on. The question of treatment is more complex. Another word for treatment is healing, which means to make people whole again. In that sense the villages are places for healing. But this healing is not a temporary activity; it is a continuous and everlasting process. And it is a healing for all living there, not only for those supposed by authorities to be deficient. The village people do not regard their villages as places for a temporary stay, but as places for life. As to the conventional meaning of treatment, the villages are clearly not places for that activity. There is no treatment for having a Down's syndrome. Through early tests and abortions one can prevent the very existence of such persons. Through facial operations one can to some extent make mongoloids look like ordinary people. The village people are against both "solutions". Instead they believe in creating communal forms which are good to live in for extraordinary people. Treatment goes on in the villages when people get sick. But not treatment against being different.

Education is also given at Vidaråsen and in the other villages. Some people learn to read and write, or knit, or play the flute or to practice eurhythmics. Most people listen to lectures or music several times every week. But that is a part of life, of everybody's life. Education is not in any way the specific purpose of the stay.

And what about care? The answer would be the same. Villages are full of care. And again it relates to everybody. Care as a part of life. But the purpose is not care. The purpose is life. On this point, however, it is more difficult to draw a line. Particularly, institutions for old folks, and for the permanently handicapped, are similar to the villages in not necessarily being temporary arrangements.

Then to a last point: Institutions have *many of the same sort of people* around. Prisoners, patients, pupils, old people, handicapped.

Is that also the case in these villages?

The answer depends on whose perspective is applied. From a conventional point of view, there are generally more of one particular sort within the limited space of the village than are found in the usual society outside the village. There are more with pensions for disabilities and many who receive financial benefits. From this point of view, therefore, villages are similar to most institutions. They have – as institutions – relatively many persons of the same sort gathered within a limited area.

But seen from the perspective of the village, the matter becomes quite different. Villagers are characters, types, personalities. They are similar because of their difference from the majority, but at the same time individually different. Institutions often extinguish differences. Sometimes numbers take the place of names, uniforms or state-provided clothes make everybody similar, and so also do compulsory haircuts and rooms or cells stripped of private belongings. In contrast to this, village life accentuates individuality and also to some extent eccentricity. From that perspective of the village the situation is therefore the opposite. It is in the external society that everybody is of the same sort, pale copies conforming to the basic demands of industrial society and its need for consumption of the products. The villages are a system where differences between individuals are allowed to develop, and where individuality reigns.

Summing it up: These villages are *similar* to institutions in having all aspects of life going on within the same limited area. Seen from the *state point of view* they are also *similar* in having many of the same sort living there. (But seen from the perspective of the villagers this aspect of the situation is the opposite.) They are also different from institutions in not being organized around a rational, specific purpose, and particularly in not accentuating any split between me and you, between us and them.

9.3 Is village life ordinary life?

Not in the statistical sense. Not if we use industrialized societies as examples of what is ordinary.

People in the villages know each other – nearly all by their first name. And the first name is used. People meet continuously. They are important to each other. They hate each other, love each other, and go out of their way to make both known. They help and hurt and care. Villages are vividly alive. They are typical tightly knit communities.

The contrast is striking when we move from villages and back to ordinary urban life. These societies are large and they are based on specialization. This creates conditions for inequality and for segregation. Also within these large types of systems there exists a mutual dependence, but that is between roles, played by easily exchangeable persons. The complex system of technical and social tools must function, but that does not depend on one person. Roles have to be filled, but performers are exchangeable. It is also in the interests of smooth functioning to make large categories similar, exchangeable. But at the same time these systems will easily consist of people foreign to each other. Most people are linked up in some sort of network. Nonetheless, the majority of those physically close to us are people we do not know.

Aliens have always existed, on the periphery of the hunter's district, outside the village, outside the small town, creating fear and anxiety. With the growth of the city a completely new situation occurred for most people. The trade-mark of the modern city is the *close alien*. The unknown ones came close, crept into the same building, but remained distant.

Compared to this type of society the villages are different. They are tightly knit. Villagers are dependent on each other, not only as roles open to everybody, but as persons. If anything, the villages are closer to mediaeval small towns than to any modern settlement. But even this does not quite fit. Seen from outside – particularly from the State's point of view – these villages contain an extraordinary number of humans who would not be able to cope with life in the ordinary society. They have in their midst an extraordinary number of those with a right to a pension, or who are in need of some sort of extraordinary assistance. Here they also differ from the prototype of the mediaeval town. Old-fashioned towns had a more even distribution of people – some of all sorts. A concentration of one sort was only found within some quarters of some towns. Such quarters were often called ghettos.

9.4 The village as a ghetto

In one interpretation of history the word Ghetto stems from the Italian word *bourghetto* – little bourg – a castle for protection or for expulsion. The old prisons grew out of the castles – some rooms deep down underground or up in a tower, a lonely view for the princess fallen from grace. Ghetto life has two aspects: persons are brought there against their will, or they gather there, for protection.

In more recent times ghettos are most closely associated with ethnicity. Italian or Chinese communities in New York, Turkish in Berlin, Scandinavian settlements for pensioners in Spain. But behind this easy use of words lingers another image, the one of shame for Europe and death for Jews. Ghettos were those parts of cities where Jews were restricted to live. It was where they had their synagogues, schools and centres of learning; it was where they worked and lived. And it was where they again and again were victims of massacres, in olden times as in recent. Killed inside the ghetto or deported to the gas chambers from the ghetto. There are not exactly good vibrations from that concept.

Nonetheless we do not change realities by shying away from words. There are people who compare the villages to ghettos. Rightly so. There are similarities, and we have to investigate. But here a dilemma comes up. If it is true that Camphill villages come close to ghettos, but ghettos give everybody bad vibrations, should we not then immediately try to disassociate the villages from that terrible word? But that would be to give Hitler and Himmler a triple victory. Then it was not only the Jews who were exterminated. Then it was not only the ghettos as physical structures, houses, shops, synagogues, which were burned. It would also mean the extermination of ghettos as a linguistic symbol for an *idea* of an important form of social life. The national socialists – and their predecessors through centuries – could kill and burn. But if we lose the concepts each time evil forces overwhelm their realities, we lose more than the battle. We lose the heritage, we lose the links to what was fine in the old idea, and eventually the ability to learn how to preserve these species. We would also desecrate the memory of those living in these forms. We have instead to rescue the idea of ghettos, find out what was their essence, see if they contain values and a framework for life which also are of importance in modern societies.

But also compared to ghettos, we find a fundamental difference when we come to the villages. Those living in Camphill villages might be seen as similar to other villagers by the State and by outsiders, but this is not the villagers' own perception. They see differences between themselves, and similarities with people in the external society. What gives villagers an identity is pride in the village as a social form, not pride due to ethnicity or any belief in being God's particular favourites.

9.5 The village as a collectivity

In the wake of the drug problems collectivities for drug users have developed. Many of them have a social form rather similar to the villages. People with drug problems and their helpers often share basic life conditions; they live together in the same households, they work together, and they take part in the same cultural activities. But there are also important differences. Collectivities have important differences between us and them. Life in the collectivities is also a planned life. Life goes on according to a treatment plan or an educational plan. Life has an explicit purpose. Those with drug problems are to reach a position where they can cope with the problem. And life in the collectivity has to come to an end. The goal is to be able to live outside the collectivity. Life in the collectivity is also supposed to be a life in progress: first year, second year, and then third year filled with trust and privileges, with clients supposed to be models for newcomers, and with persons nearly ripe for life in the ordinary society.

Only a minority actually stays on until the last stage. Some of those who stay, and also some of those who run away earlier, sometimes declare that they actually would have wanted to stay on, maybe mostly using it as a base to come back to, but in some cases forever. These express a longing for the collective form, for the ideals, for the communal living. Some also make it; they come back as staff.

Seen from the perspective of the villages the major problem with the collectives is exactly what some of these youngsters express. Life in a good social system becomes somehow unreal when it is only for treatment or training, and with a definite end. From the good life, appealing to ideals and mobilizing warm social relations, those living there are pushed back into forms of social life which are far from collective and with an emotional temperature on quite another level. From the village perspective it seems natural to suggest that collectivities are a good thing, but that they should never come to a forced end. Those who want to stay on should do so forever.

Impossible, would be the answer from society and also from many workers in the collectivities. Then the whole thing would choke, there would be no empty places for new drug addicts. But again, from the village perspective, one would suggest the obvious solution: Let new people create new collectivities. The old ones would probably slowly be able to earn more money and need slightly reduced support from the social welfare system. Generation after generation of new addicts might thus be able to move into new collective systems. Drugs would then really be a powerful factor in shaping the social fabric of a country.

But again a statement on the impossibility would come, this time maybe particularly from professional circles. If collectivities were not for treatment, what then with the treaters? What about professional standards, case-loads, utility and knowledge of how to bring it all to an end? If the master-plan and utility thinking collapsed, and if the clear goal collapsed, and if the role as clients collapsed, then also the professional role would collapse. Then only ordinary standards for life would be left in the collectivities.

So, it will not happen. But if it had happened, then the present collectivities would have been social systems close to what the Camphill villages are today.

9.6 The village as a village

To understand what villages are, an attempt has been made – I hope with care and concern – to describe these tender species. Then an attempt has been made to understand even more by comparing villages to other social arrangements. Total institutions have been one. We found some important similarities, but also basic dissimilarities. Our villages are not institutions, and therefore not total institutions either, but they are more total than the ordinary society. More close to our villages were ghettos and collectivities, but here too fundamental differences remained.

What then is a village?

I am tempted to answer in the words of the Greek poet, Konstantin Kavafis (1961), in his description of the road to Ithaka:

> Pray that your road's a long one
> Keep Ithaka always in mind
> Arriving there is what you're destined for
> But don't hurry the journey at all
> Better if it goes on for years
> so you're old by the time you reach the island
> wealthy with all you have gained on the way
> not expecting Ithaka to make you rich
> Ithaka gave you the marvellous journey
> without her you wouldn't have set out
> She hasn't anything else to give

The Camphill villages have something from all these other types of social systems, but they are also different from them all. They are peculiar. So peculiar that we have no general concept for them, no word in common use which immediately tells most people what they are.

A communal life, with many of one sort together, without other goals than life and understanding, for such a life we are without immediately understood concepts ready for use. So, let us accept to call them just villages.

Villages are no part of the Norwegian heritage. In a land mostly filled with stone the distances between the fields were so large that households were forced to settle apart from each other. Also when it comes to Central European villages, it can be doubted if these today belong to the same species as the villages described in this book. The old villages come closer, even if they had their class differences and their rulers within and from without. But they also had qualities of cultural life and cohesion, close to what is found within Vidaråsen and the other places. Modern life has extinguished villages as a major form of social organization. Maybe the extraordinary needs of the extraordinary people will help to re-establish a model of a social form which probably is good for most people. Maybe the extraordinary ones might initiate a push towards at least an intellectual debate on how to convert parts of cities into conglomerates of more or less independent villages.

10

The Long Way Home

Sometimes I ask my students how they would behave on entering a bus. Only two seats are empty, both in front. One is close to a man who looks as most men look. The other is close to one obviously different from most men. By officials he might be called retarded, or maybe insane. Which seat do you, or we, choose?

10.1 De-institutionalization

The catchword in recent times has been de-institutionalization. Italy made an early start by closing down institutions for the insane. Patients should come out of the hospitals and go back to society. The United States made an early start with youth prisons. A new director, shocked by what he saw, sold off the institutions so there were no alternatives to letting the youngsters go.[1] In Scandinavia institutions for troublesome vagrants have all gone. So have also many of the special schools or other places for physically and mentally handicapped persons. Again and again scandals disrupted the trust in these institutions. Today, the major course is to get all sorts of people out of institutions and into the ordinary system of schools, of health service and of welfare. Basically, all are to live the ordinary life in the ordinary society.

It sounds fine, until one looks into that ordinary society.

The Italian females were among the first to protest. The insane back to the families was the slogan, but those families were not the same as when they left. They were not large any more; they did not provide free service from females permanently at home. The road from the mental hospital did not lead to a home filled with life and vivacity. The road led with great regularity to a room

---

1 Jerome Miller is soon to publish a book on why and how he did it.

in a boarding house in the centre of the city. Or it led to an existence as a bag-lady, homeless and with all belongings in some plastic bags, strolling the streets of our glittering, modern towns. Or it led to another type of institution – to prison.

Landscapes of despair are often where they end. Dear and Wolch (1987) have given a vivid description of the road from de-institutionalization to homelessness, and also of the particular dangers that now become visible. Those without good alternatives tend to end up in the centre of the large cities. Here most of the welfare-workers are available. Here are also rooming-houses and a general tolerance towards these types of people. Nice neighbourhoods will not have them; the suburbanites close ranks. The centres of cities are often a bit run down, relatively sparsely inhabited, with room for those who are different. Here they move in and create some sort of segregated quarters.

But they are vulnerable. And these quarters come to an end almost before they have got started. All over the industrialized world the same social process is taking place: Inner cities are becoming popular again. There is no more space available on the outskirts of the cities. At the same time it is becoming more attractive both to live and to work in the centre. The contaminating factories have moved far out, or been converted into clean, electronic industry. Urban renewal puts its stamp on the town. Central town is also central to live in. A process of gentrification takes place. For those living in the segregated quarters it is a catastrophe. They do not belong among the beautiful people, and slowly they are pushed out. The city centres become too good for them. But suburban areas have not changed in the meantime; they will not receive them. Therefore, as in mediaeval times they are pushed out on to the roads, from town to town, hunting for cheap space for cheap living. In this process they will often come into contact with the forces of law and order. From being troublesome they are re-defined as being criminal. Prisons take over where institutions for care were dissolved and the inner city beautified.

This situation is not without exceptions. De-institutionalization has often meant a real improvement. Young people escaped the brutalizing effects of youth-prisons. Clients have been moved out of closed institutions and into local communities. The Italian experiment was not the total failure that defenders of the old psychiatry like to claim. Former inmates have often received their own apartments, living alone or with a few others of the same sort. If help is needed, some professional comes around, with advice on social matters, with a helping hand in treatment, or concretely with food and clean clothes. Sometimes some helpers sleep in the apartment or house, or nearby, available if trouble threatens. It is a reality that lots of people have been brought out of institutions and back to more ordinary surroundings.

From schools we also get stories of success. Children who in the old days went to special schools, are now admitted into the ordinary ones. In some cases extra teachers help them through in the ordinary classes. In other cases they are gathered in special classes designed for their needs. Often they have a good time, taking part in school and in social life. People learn to know them. Some of the mysticism around them disappears. Particularly in the countryside they become known to the community and will probably get an easier life than they would have had if they had not been in the ordinary school.

But schools also have seats for choice, as in buses. Life among children is a rough life. Choices are not at random. Teachers can arrange, parents can encourage, but in vital situations those who are more different than most will find themselves alone. If there are several of them in the school, they will tend to find each other. Grudgingly, because their rejecting friends' criteria are also theirs. But they have no alternative. In schools where they are alone, they remain alone. Why should ordinary children behave differently from ordinary grown-ups?

Adults in need of help are helped into apartments. The message is in the word. A parte – to one side, appartare – to separate. A rough day, home from work, your own key, you open the door, it locks behind you. You are alone. A blessing for people in need of letting pretences go.

But those of particular concern in this book are maybe back from a place of work where they have also been the last social choices. They have been in the bus as described. They have had this experience through years of rejections. Now they are alone, or with two or three other rejects in an apartment, – their separate part.

They remain alone unless there are some hired helpers there during parts of the day or unless there are some others to stay with them during the night. And often there are, but with two built-in problems. The one is cost. Welfare states are generally in trouble and increasingly so. Welfare states were created within nations where a majority had experienced or lived close to scarcity. But that is a majority on its way out. At the same time costs are soaring. The extra money given to those with extra needs is not so easily available any more.

The other problem is less obvious. It has to do with the qualities of social life based on payment.

10.2 Paid friends?

Through de-institutionalization some of the people in need of help are back to ordinary society, but in a special way. They are, but they are not. It is as if an invisible wall of glass exists between them and us. They are in our streets, our buses, our schools, in our houses and places of work. Close, but distant; among us, but lonely.

The major solution for those brought back from the institutions, or not placed there any longer, is to build up a supporting network. It is generally accepted that the ordinary society is not what is was. Households are smaller, relatives live so far apart that mutual assistance in care is complicated; people with extraordinary needs for help and assistance are in extraordinarily big trouble.

Help is needed. And help is provided. An army of professional helpers is mobilized. In day time, in afternoon time, in the nights. Hours after hours of paid help. The growth in the number of social workers and related professionals has been fabulous. But the people of particular interest to us are lonely people. And then comes the question: Can we train a profession to cope with these tasks? Can we train them just to be available in a role close to friendship or close to being a relative? What sort of training, what sort of wage demands? Can we create a profession to cope with loneliness?

We provide a network of helpers. Paid, full-time helpers or voluntary helpers under the supervision of the full-timers. Both have it in common that the need for help is the reason for the interaction. They relate to the person they help because of needs in that person. This is similar to a situation when parents care for children, or lovers for the one of them who gets sick, similar, but not identical. Children are more to their parents than persons in need of help. Lovers have a broad relationship in matters far away from sickness and need. The one being helped is in most cases only temporarily in a weak position; this in contrast to the professionalized situation where the imbalance is a permanent condition.

What also typifies ordinary social life, is diffuseness in rights and obligations between parties. In contrast to this, professionals and their voluntary helpers are trained to draw lines and to specify obligations. For professionals, continuously being approached by new persons in need of help, it is important to draw these lines and to specify obligations. Rules are drawn as to how close the receiver of help is to be admitted, on how to keep up barriers against intimacy, and on limits of time allocated to any particular person.

In sum, the relationship between the helper and the person to be helped will exhibit two important special features when the helper is a professional or a quasi-professional. It will be a relationship out of balance in the sense that the one is permanently the giver and the other the receiver. And it will be a relationship with emphasis on clear specifications of the responsibilities of the giver. Both features are basically different from those found in friendship, where equality between the friends is one of the pillars and the other is lack of any limits in the obligation to stand up for the friend.

10.3 The sower

The sower can be seen as a symbol of established ideas in modern social policy. No institutions. No segregation. No enclaves of extraordinary people. Everybody back to ordinary society. The ideal is that those in trouble are to be spread out, as evenly as seeds on the fields in early spring. Instead of gathering many of the extraordinary ones within one limited area, they are spread out thin, with extraordinary possibilities to come close to ordinary people, but at the same time, with extraordinary lack of possibilities for being with people with the same trouble as themselves.

People in need of help are to some extent untouched by the ordinary society, that society where they are spread out thin. Instead they are soaked into the extraordinary society, the society of paid helpers. They do not easily get friends, and their equals are few and far between, difficult to find, and therefore of limited so-

cial importance. The paid helpers are the major alternative to mi-
sery and complete loneliness. Instead of diffuse, egalitarian relationship, they enter specific subordinate positions in a system created to care for them. Instead of becoming friends, they become
clients.

10.4 Clientization of minorities

The strength in this process can be illustrated by what sometimes
happens to refugees or immigrants within welfare states influenced by the idea of the sower. They are often spread out thin.
An upper limit is set to the number accepted within an area. This
is supposed to help assimilation, particularly for those most alien.
A thin layer of refugees all over the country after the second
world war. And in these days a sprinkling of Latin-Americans,
Kurds, Africans or Iranians, from Kristiansand in the south and
up north to the Russian border, which is a distance as long as from
Oslo to Africa. Here they are supposed to live, with miles between them, under the hypothesis that this will give them fast access to the ordinary Norwegian society.

Of course, they flee this situation. Being people with resources
enough to fly their country of birth when life there turned impossible, many among them also have resources to fly the internal
exile they are forced into in their new country. They do what they
are supposed not to. They congregate. They leave their nice
apartments all over the country and gather where they find other
people. They ignore all sorts of hardships, live in quarters below
dignity, all to be close to people of their own sort. In theory they
ought to be dependent, clients. With all that sort of hardship they
are supposed to become a burden on the state system of support.
In reality it is the other way round. As Beckert and Lönnrot
(1988) show from Denmark, the very fact that they are together
with their own folks, makes it possible for them to survive. They
get into numerous mutual relationships with people of shared destiny. They help each other, on equal terms. They become ordinary, associative people, not clients. But it is a solution in disson-
ance with the principle of the sower. It is against equality.

10.5 Natural enclaves

If they are strong enough, ethnic minorities try to come close to each other. But not all. Some will cross the wall and become ordinary. After a while whole enclaves will dissolve and all members cross the wall. Finns in Sweden are an example. They strive to keep their Finnish language, but it is difficult. Finns and Swedes have the same basic goals, work and money – that's why the Finns came. Except for language it is unclear how they differ, and especially whether the immigrants have anything particularly worth defending through living together (Rosenberg 1987). Often assimilation seems to go faster if the first few years in a new country take place among equals. Israel tried first to build its nation on the principle of the sower, but changed later. Those from one nation were encouraged to commence together and then slowly move into the greater mixture. US is a prime example of this, but also of immigrants who stay in their enclaves if they are numerous enough. Minnesota is still filled with Norwegian settlements who traditionally hate the Swedes thirty miles further up.

Ordinary people construct social life so that they can find their own sort around. Maybe not so ordinary people ought to do the same?

They are not allowed to. Many of the same sort of people in need of help, that is what one found in an institution. Or worse, it is called a ghetto.

This illustrates our basic dilemma: Insane people, lonely people, people called mentally retarded, or shy people, they are lonely in our societies. They are lonely as so many others are lonely, only more so. They can be helped, but become clients. Or they can be given the possibility to help each other. But then they remain different, outside the usual. The dilemma is this: Is it better to be spread out – thin – among the usual people, close to them, not a full-fledged member, but helped to be there, near to ordinary life, a normal life, but life as a client? Or is it better to be among the unordinary, handicapped by not living as those in the major solution, but not lonely and not as a client?

10.6 The deaf and dumb

Berit is a good student, living with her friend, a normal couple, a normal life. She is furious when the topic "many extraordinary people living together" is mentioned. She is weak-sighted and lived like that for a long time: In one big house, in company with mostly blind people, trained to do what blind people were supposed to do; switchboard-operator was to be her destiny, until she broke away from it all and became as most people. She would not live there, confined to the company of people of her own sort, a dependent, a client.

But Berit might have been deaf, from birth on. Growing up alone might in that situation have meant an extraordinary amount of isolation. With no other deaf persons around the chances would be high that she would be considered mentally retarded. Without hearing she would not learn to talk. With those close to her she might have developed a rudimentary system of communication. With resources in the family she might have been sent away to an educational institution for the deaf and dumb. Dumb means simply stupid, with linguistic roots back to something filled with dark smoke.

Would Berit – if deaf – have been better off in a school for the deaf and dumb? The chances are great that she would. Not necessarily because of teachers, but because of the other children there. They were also deaf and supposedly dumb, but less so the more they come together. Being there, with a shared handicap, they did what all humans do when given the opportunity; they developed alternatives. To communicate is a primary urge in humans. Deprived of the usual means, humans develop unusual ones. Deaf children develop sign language. They develop a language based on positions and movements of fingers, hands, lips and body. By being together, they overcome their limitations.

But against this solution come the integrationists. They claim that the deaf are to be helped out of their segregated living. Or, if help is not enough, they are to be forced out. The way of forcing them is to dissolve institutions, discourage the use of sign language and give them individual training in lip-reading and also in talking.

So here are two world views. One that looks at deaf people as belonging to a minority culture with a language for themselves, but therefore – as with all cultural minorities – with a need for each other. The other looks at deafness as a deep handicap that needs to be overcome. To do so it is necessary to dissolve their culture, extinguish their language and to the utmost get the deaf people into the mainstream of ordinary life.

The war between these two world views raged with particular intensity in the USA around the turn of the century. The major carrier of the view that the deaf belonged to a minority culture and ought to do so, was a Frenchman, *Laurent Clerc*. He was deaf himself, came from the famous National Institution for the Deaf in Paris, an institution solidly based on sign language. To come to this institution from his village was like coming from a cave "in which the shadow of meaning had flickered, cryptic and ominous, on the gray walls; I came out into the bright day of true communication, where a message was no sooner expressed than understood." (Lane 1984, p. 10).

But his antagonist had more power. This man could hear. He had a beautiful voice and a brilliant mind. This was Alexander Graham Bell, the inventor of the telephone. His interest for deaf people did not come from his inventions, it was the other way round, but it was an invention in harmony with his intense struggle against sign language. Again in the words of Lane (1984, pp. 340–341):

> Clerc and Bell were opposed not only in the central cause to which they devoted their lives, in their historical roles, but in virtually every other way. Where Clerc found strength in human variety, Bell found weakness and danger. Where Clerc saw difference, Bell saw deviance. The one had a social model of atypical people, the other a medical model. For Clerc, deafness was, above all, a social disability, the great problem of the deaf was the hearing world in which they were a minority; he hoped for a day when hearing people of goodwill would remove the handicap by accepting deaf culture and language. For Bell, deafness was a physical handicap; if it could not be cured, it could be alleviated by covering its stigmata; hearing people of goodwill would aid the deaf in a denial of their particular language and culture, in "passing" as hearing people in a hearing world. Addressing a conference of speech teachers, Bell said of deaf children, "We should try ourselves to forget that they are deaf. We should teach them to forget that they are deaf."

While for Clerc the overriding purpose of education was personal fulfilment, for Bell it was integration with the hearing majority:

> I admit . . . the ease with which a deaf child acquires this sign language and its perfect adaptability for the purpose of developing his mind; but after all, it is not the language of the millions of people among whom his lot in life is cast." Clerc favoured deaf teachers for the model they provided to the children, for their zeal, and for their own personal fulfilment, but Bell opposed them as an obstacle to integration. Clerc saw the signing community as an indigenous linguistic minority, and linguistic scholarship of the last few decades bears him out, for it has discovered many respects in which American Sign Language partakes of apparently universal properties of human language. Bell views the deaf as one of the defective classes, among which he counted the blind and the mentally retarded. Clerc saw merit in congregation of the deaf – in couples, for compatibility; in schools, for mutual instruction by peers; in gatherings, for communal reflection and social action. Bell saw evil in marriage among the deaf, residential schools, and social organizations.
>
> For Clerc, an immigrant and polyglot, bilingualism was a worthy goal for deaf and hearing persons alike. Every deaf person should learn to write at least essentials in the national language and the highly educated deaf, spokespersons for a community with no written language, should master that of the majority; he himself had done so. Bell, on the contrary, favored monolingualism for all Americans. Speaking to the National Education Association, he said, "Our population is recruited from all countries of the world and from this source another danger threatens the republic. It is important for the preservation of our national existence that the people of this country should speak one tongue."

And the superior value of speaking was beyond discussion for Bell. Lane describes (p. 365) how Bell reacted when a conference of principals meeting in Minnesota placed on its agenda the question "What is the importance of speech to the deaf?" Bell was flabbergasted: "I am astonished. I am pained. To ask the value of speech? It is like asking the value of life! . . ."

Rarely is the dilemma of integration illustrated so well as in the history of deafness. Bell realized that no language was more useful to the deaf than the sign language. But that could not be the main view because "the main object of the education of the deaf is to fit them to live in the world of hearing-speaking people." This is a parallel to what other integrationists state: The main object is to fit them to live in the world of ordinary people. It is just. What is good for me, is *good. And good for all.*

"And the silence fell," are the final words in Lane's book. Bell got his way. Those born deaf lost their language.

While I was writing this in Norway, a revolution took place among the deaf in the USA. I did not learn about it before this book was about ready, and then through an article by Oliver Sacks (1988).

The revolution he describes was a freedom fight. It took place at Gallaudet, the only liberal art college for the deaf in the USA. This college traced its roots back to Clerc and sign language, but had for a long time suffered from the suppression of sign language. Now came a change, a re-legitimation and resurrection of sign language as never before, everywhere, except in the administration and within the board of trustees. Now the college was to have a new president. Six candidates were available, three hearing, three deaf. Three thousand persons gathered to make it clear that teachers as well as students wanted a deaf president. But the board of trustees refused to listen and selected a hearing president. A week of vigorous protests followed. The new president took a tough stand. But deaf people all over the USA joined in the protest, the pressure became immense, the president of one week succumbed this time with grace, and a deaf person was at last given the position. The campaign was in itself of importance. Sacks quotes one participant (p. 24):

> I'm from a hearing family . . . My whole life I've felt pressures, hearing pressures on me – "You can't do it in the hearing world, you can't make it in the hearing world" – and right now all pressure is lifted from me. I feel free, all of a sudden, full of energy now. The words "deaf and dumb" will be destroyed forever; instead there'll be "deaf and able".
>
> The campaign was directed against misdirected paternalism, which, the deaf feel, is anything but benign – based as it is on pity and condescension, and on an implicit view of them as "incompetent", if not diseased. Special objection has been made to some of the doctors involved in Gallaudet's affairs, who, it is felt, tend to see the deaf merely as having diseased ears, and not as a whole people adapted to another sensory mode.

Sacks underlines that the suppression of sign language in the 1880s had a deleterious effect on the deaf for 75 years, not only on their education and academic achievements, but on their image of themselves and on their entire community and culture.

Deaf culture is reared upon deaf nature, though at this point one almost has an impulse to drop the word "deaf", and replace it with "visual", and to speak rather of an intensely visual culture emerging from a physiological enhancement of visuality.

Why did they succeed this time? Sacks suggests an explanation through a quotation from one of the leaders in the protest:

> It's really remarkable, because in all my experience I've seen deaf people be passive and accept the kind of treatment that hearing people give them. I've seen them willing, or seem to be willing, to be "clients", when in fact they should be controlling things . . .
>   I don't understand what you mean by "clients", I say.
>   You know Tim Rarus [Bob explains] – the one you saw at the barricades this morning, whose signing you so admired as pure and passionate – well, he summoned up in two words what this transformation is all about. He said: "It's very simple. No deaf president, no university." . . . That was the first time deaf people ever realized that a colonial client-industry like this can't exist without the client. It's a billion-dollar industry for hearing people. If deaf people don't participate, the industry is gone.

There are some similarities between the deaf and those in the centre of attention in this book. The deaf lost their language. Silence fell. But isolated people also stop talking. For many, with biological equipment at variance to the majority, it is a pre-condition for their communication that their social life takes place within forms where they can use their communicative abilities to the utmost. They need *permanency* in relationships so that common meaning in non-verbal symbols can be built up. All sorts of temporary helpers to temporary welfare workers is the worst possible solution. They need less competing noise, so that their signals can be received. They need more tolerance both for unexpected behaviour and for that which is only too expected. They need what most people need.

Living a Normal Life

11.1 Villages in towns

An attempt was quite recently made to create a Camphill village in the middle of Oslo. The intention was to create a village for those who are different, a village similar to those described in this book. The reasoning behind the proposal was simple. Most people who live in the villages are from towns. It is not right that they shall leave their place of birth. It is not right for them. Villages ought to exist where people come from. And it is not right for the towns. It would not have been right that they were allowed to export what they see as their problems. But in reality the situation is the opposite, so my argument runs: The towns lose their extraordinary people. It is not right for the towns that they are allowed to lose what might prove important resources.

Because of all this, the time was seen as ripe to take the next step in the village movement. Villages have to be made in the middle of the cities. A suitable place was found, a quadrangle of houses from the nineteenth century, surrounding a green field. Each floor in the houses could provide room for a group of the size that usually live together within the houses in the villages. Some houses might be converted into workshops. The special needs of the city might provide increased opportunities for work. A hostel could be operated for a nearby hospital. A repair workshop for bicycles, a day centre for people with problems living in other areas of the city, – and then a meeting room for huge gatherings, for the usual lectures, concerts, village meetings, etc. There would be problems due to the proximity to the troubled city. But there would also be gains. With a strong social milieu inside the village they would become centres rather than peripheral. The villagers would become hosts for people seeking their company, rather than guests hunting for company in the external city. Together people with troubles would be able to explore the city, its markets and museums, its parks, theatres and other public arenas. It would have aspects of ghetto-life, but one with extraordinarily strong contact to the external city.

This was the plan. It functioned as a provocation. There exists an Association for the benefit of the mentally retarded. The membership consists mainly of relatives of those supposed to be retarded. The president of the Oslo association wrote: This is a proposal which encourages segregation and special care. A village in the town would mean that mentally retarded persons should be shielded against living a normal life with all the experiences of that life. But clearly, she adds, the conditions must be created so that they – with their special problems – can lead a life full of meaning. (From *Vår rett*, No. 3 1988, p 10–11.)

This view was also conveyed officially to the Ministry of Social Affairs. Shortly afterwards the answer came. With explicit reference to the views of the association for the mentally retarded, any assistance to create a village inside the city was refused. Renewed approaches directly to municipal authorities in Oslo proved equally vain. According to a plan unanimously agreed upon recently by the Norwegian parliament, all institutions for the mentally retarded are to be disposed of within a few years. The institutions were found below dignity. The municipalities are instead made responsible for bringing "their" clients back home. A considerable amount of money (in 1990 NOK 500,000 per client per year, which is approximately 50,000 pounds sterling) is granted by the state to enable the municipalities to do this. Up to the moment of printing this book, those particularly responsible for helping people out of institutions and back to society in the capital have refused even to discuss the idea of a village in town.

11.2 Right or duty

Most of us have made it. We are able to function within the major social arrangements. We choose company and are chosen. We oscillate, in and out, and in again. To those who are chosen, privacy is a good thing. But the very term has a double meaning. It means to be free, but also to deprive, rob. For someone without access to cars, highways throughout the community might reduce qualities of life. For others, emphasis on privacy might have the same effects. Those others might even be many. But they are not in an easy position to explain this, they are not close to the public arena for communication.

The extraordinary people have their friends and their association of friends. These friends are "ordinary". And they think in terms of justice. Why should not those in need of help lead the same life as all people? What is good for us ought to be available for too. It feels like a deception not to make that life into a life for all.

In addition comes the provocation of village life. At least to me, that life has created doubts regarding the fundamental arrangements of the life I live in and with. The village societies challenge fundamental premises of ordinary life. It is obviously a life with qualities for many in need of help. But *most people* are in need of help; when young, when hit by a crisis, or maybe permanently. Help in coping with life problems, with loneliness, with inability to cope with money – not least inability to balance needs for money with ideals of giving it away. Maybe those in villages live a better life than anybody outside. Maybe we all ought to live in villages. Ideas like this threaten the very base of everyday life. It becomes an additional reason for rejection of the idea of villages for extraordinary people.

To talk about the right of living an ordinary life becomes too simple. It is not only a question of rights, but of obligations to live that life. It is not only concerned with equality for all, but with a cultural hegemony protecting the major solutions of industrialized society. These villages represent alternatives so challenging that they are rejected.

11.3 Two honourable words

Assimilation is one of these words. It means what it says: To make similar, like everyone else. Extraordinary people are not.

Integration is the other, and maybe of even higher and undisputed rank within all movements to get the extraordinary people into the ordinary society as ordinary members. When asked what it means, many have an answer. A correct answer. One folded his hands, now they are integrated. Others said forming a whole, emerging into the whole, becoming a part of the totality. Some point to integration as the opposite of segregation. No wonder that it has become an honourable word, the goal to be attained in all work for those supposed to be handicapped.

But words often have double meanings, reflecting deep dilemmas. Going further back in the history of the very key concept for the advocates of a normal life, we find another root. In the history of words integration has developed out of *tangere*, which means touch. The prefix "in" is a negation. In-tegration, therefore, means non-touched. That meaning is quite clear when we talk about a person "of integrity". People not touched are integrated people.

Extraordinary people are not similar to other people, and can never be. They can be given more help than ordinary people, in the belief that this will compensate for what are seen as defects, and create an end result similar to that of others. But as described, this help is in our recent way of thinking given in the form of paid friendship. Total assimilation is, therefore, an impossibility. The more one is helped to become similar, the more one is made to become a client, which literally means one who comes when the lord calls. To be a client is not to be integrated in the sense of being one finger in the folded hand or a part of a totality similar to everyone else.

It is more realistic to work towards integration in the archaic meaning of that concept. No humans can survive completely integrated, completely untouched. It is through the tender and sometimes not so tender touches from other humans one becomes one of them. But there are limits to the benefits of being touched, as well as there are limits to the possibilities of surviving without being touched. People who are different might profit from social forms where they are protected from being made into clients. The villages are one among several possible examples of such social forms. By tuning in to the specific abilities and needs among the exceptional people, we might be able to create viable alternatives to the major solutions of industrialized society. In the end we might find it beneficial for most of us to live in social forms considered particularly suitable for the exceptional people.

Bibliography

Beckert, Birgitte and Gitte Lönnrot: "Etniske grupper og bosætning." ("Ethnic Groups and Habitation"). *Information*, Copenhagen March 21, 1988. Cfr. also: Nils Ufer: *Set fra Ishøj*. Copenhagen 1988.

Dear, Michael and Jennifer Wolch: *Landscapes of Despair: From Deinstitutionalization to Homelessness*. Oxford 1987.

Edgerton, Robert B.: *The Clock of Competence: Stigma in the lives of the Mentally Retarded*. Berkeley 1967.

Ekelöf, Gunnar: *Blandade kort. (Mixed cards)*. Stockholm 1957.

Ende, Michael: *The Never-Ending Story*. London 1984.

Foucault, Michel: *Discipline and Punish: The Birth of the Prison*. London 1977.

Foucault, Michel: *Madness and Civilization: A History of Insanity in the Age of Reason*. London 1965.

Goffman, Erving: *Essays on the Social Situation of Mental Patients and Other Inmates*. New York 1961.

Illich, Ivan: *Tools for Conviviality*. New York and London 1973.

Kavafis, Konstantin (or Kabaphis, Konstantinos): *The Complete Poems*. New York 1961.

König, Karl: *The Camp Hill movement*. Camphill Press, Great Britain 1960.

Lane, Harlan: *When the Mind Hears: A History of the Deaf*. New York and Toronto 1984.

Leinslie, Gjertrud: "Beretning fra et verksted". ("Account from a Workshop"). Vidaråsen 1984.

Rosenberg, Thomas: *På spaning efter en ny tydelighet. (Searching for a New Clarity)*. Hangö, Finland 1987.

Rudeng, Erik: "Robert Owen". *Pax Lexikon*, Vol. 5, Oslo 1980.

Sachs, Oliver: "The Revolution of the Deaf 1988". *New York Review of Books*, June 2 1988.

Seip, Didrik Arup: *Hjemme og i fiendeland. (At Home and on Hostile Territory)*. Oslo 1946.

Steiner, Rudolf: *Antroposophy and the Social Question*. 1905, New York 1982.

Ufer, Nils: *Set fra Ishøj. (Seen from Ishøj)*. Copenhagen 1988.

Zborowski, Mark and Elizabeth Herzog: *Little-Town of Eastern Europe*. New York 1952.

Østerberg, Dag: *Fortolkende sosiologi. (An Interpreting Sociology)*. Oslo 1986.

Østerberg, Dag: *Metasociology: An Inquiry into the Origins and Validity of Social Thought*. Oslo 1988.

Suggested Reading on Camphill Villages

Allen, Joane de Deris: *Living Buildings: Expressing Fifty Yeas of Camphill.* Aberdeen 1989. (To be published).

König, Karl: *In Need of Special Understanding.* Botton Village, Danby North Yorkshire, 1986.

König, Karl: *The Camphill Movement.* Botton Village, Danby, North Yorkshire, 1960.

Parmann, Øystein: "Vidaråsen Landsby: Ideer – dagligliv – bakgrunn." ("The Vidaråsen Commune: Ideas – Daily life – Background"). Oslo 1980.

Pietzner, Cornelius M.: *Village Life: The Camphill Communities.* Salzburg 1986.

Pietzner, Cornelius M.: *Aspects of Curative Education.* Aberdeen 1966.

Pietzner, Cornelius M.: *Candle on the Hill: The Camphill Communities Worldwide.* Edinburgh 1989. (To be published).

Steiner, Rudolf: *The Social Future.* 1919, Spring Valley, New York 1972.

Steiner, Rudolf: *Towards Social Renewal. Basic Issues of the Social Question.* 1961, London 1977.

Weihs, Anke and Joan Tallø, revised ed. by Wain Farrants: *Camphill Villages.* Botton Village, Danby North Yorkshire 1988.

Weihs, Thomas: *Children in Need of Special Care.* London 1977.